GRAND CANYON

COOK BOOK

*Southwestern recipes from
Arizona's natural wonder!*

Bobbi and Bruce Fischer

**Golden
WEST☼
PUBLISHERS**

Front cover photo by Dick Dietrich
Back cover photos courtesy of El Tovar, Grand Canyon National Park Lodges
Inside illustrations by Sean Hoy

Library of Congress Cataloging-in-Publication Data

Fischer, Bobbi, 1947-
The Grand Canyon Cook Book / Bobbi Fischer & Bruce Fischer.
   p.   cm.
Includes index.
1. Cookery, American—Southwestern Style. 2. Grand Canyon
Region (Ariz.)—Description and travel. I. Fischer, Bruce, 1958–
   II. Title.
ISBN 13: 978-1-885590-20-6
ISBN 10: 1-885590-20-2
TX715.2.S69S25 1997   96-50003
641.5979—dc21   CIP

Manufactured by Friesens Corporation in Altona, Canada
November 2009
Job 50769

Golden West Publishers
(a division of American Traveler Press)
5738 North Central Avenue
Phoenix, AZ 85012-1316
800-521-9221

For free sample recipes from every Golden West cookbook, visit:
www.goldenwestpublishers.com

The
GRAND CANYON COOK BOOK
Table of Contents

About the Canyon

About the Authors

Bruce and Bobbi Fischer are avid hikers and have been visiting the Grand Canyon since 1979. They have traveled the Southwest hiking and collecting recipes for many years, and they continue to search for interesting recipes and food trivia.

Bruce is a professional musician and videographer and a native of Phoenix, Arizona. Originally from Boston, Bobbi is a family therapist in Scottsdale, Arizona. They have authored four other cookbooks, *Cowboy Cook Book, Tortilla Lovers Cook Book, Western Breakfasts* and *Utah Cook Book*.

Bruce and Bobbi have also collaborated to write and produce several children's activity books.

Special Note: If you have a favorite recipe that represents your memory of the Grand Canyon, please send it to the authors via Golden West Publishers, 5738 North Central Avenue, Phoenix, AZ 85012-1316. They may include it in their next cookbook!

Introduction

What draws more than five million visitors to the Grand Canyon each year?

The Canyon has lured visitors since its discovery. The adventuresome have flocked to the Grand Canyon since the 1800s, sharing their experiences with each other and with their families and friends throughout the world.

Every time we gaze upon its steeples and spires we surrender our imagination to the Canyon's awe-some power. We have found that each person develops their own personal relationship with the Grand Canyon.

As veteran hikers, we too have had the good fortune of sharing our experiences with others and enjoying the feeling of community that exists among the Canyon's visitors. Our talks with hikers, visitors, rangers and residents have led to this compilation of recipes. Certain recipes bring back memories of a trail, viewpoint or lodge experience. We hope *The Grand Canyon Cook Book* brings back wonderful memories of your Canyon experience, or maybe entices you to experience the Canyon for yourself, if you have not yet done so.

We invite you to recreate the tantalizing tastes and enjoy the alluring folklore and adventures of the Grand Canyon through this collection of our favorite recipes from the North and South Rims.

Bobbi and Bruce Fischer

Havasupai Indians

For centuries, the Havasupai Indians have been the only Native Americans living in the Grand Canyon. They make their home in Havasu Canyon near the blue-green waters of Havasu Creek for which they are named. Havasupai means "people of the blue-green water".

When Father Francisco Tomás Garcés ventured north from San Xavier del Bac Mission in southern Arizona, to seek new converts, he came upon these native people farming the land. The Havasupai treated Garcés as royalty, but he soon left when he found that he was unable to convert them to his religion.

When reservation land was established for Native Americans in the 1880s, Havasupai Chief Ko-hot helped establish an area within the Grand Canyon to sustain his People.

The Havasupai farmed the land, harvesting corn, melons, beans and squash. A portion of their crops was dried and stored in sealed caves in the canyon cliff walls, just as the People had done for almost 1,000 years.

If you hike down to Havasu Canyon, you will see the stone pillars above the village of Supai. Legend boasts that the village was erected here because of the "wigeleeva" (stone pillars). These pillars were believed to be protective spirits that watched over the People and their crops.

As you recreate some of the recipes in *The Grand Canyon Cook Book* containing corn, beans, squash or melons, take time to reflect on the historic significance of these crops and the people who have been sustained by them for hundreds of years.

Appetizers

Jalapeño Delights

1 lb. **Sharp Cheddar Cheese**, shredded
1 can (4 oz.) **Jalapeños**, diced
1 medium **Onion**, chopped
3 cloves **Garlic**
1/2 cup **Mayonnaise**
1 cup chopped **Piñon Nuts**
Tortilla Chips

Combine cheese, jalapeños (diced), onion and garlic in blender. Add mayonnaise and blend until smooth. Chill until firm. Form into one large ball or 16-20 bite-size balls. Chill until cheese balls are firm. Remove from refrigerator and roll in nuts. Return to refrigerator until ready to serve with your favorite tortilla chips.

Pico de Gallo

A great appetizer with tortilla chips
and can be used as a topping for main dishes, too!

4 small **Jalapeños**, diced
1 can (4 oz.) **Diced Green Chiles**
3 large **Tomatoes**, diced
1/4 cup diced **Black Olives**
1/8 cup diced **Onion**
1/4 cup diced **Green Bell Pepper**
1/2 tsp. **Salt**
1 tsp. **Garlic Powder**

Mix the jalapeños, chiles, tomatoes, olives, onion and bell pepper in a large mixing bowl. Add the salt and garlic powder. Place mixture in a bright, decorative serving bowl and put in refrigerator for one hour.

Coyote Cheese Log

1 pkg. (8 oz.) **Processed Cheese**, softened
1 pkg. (3 oz.) **Cream Cheese**, softened
1/4 tsp. **Garlic Powder**
1 tbsp. **Lemon Juice**
Ground Red Pepper, to taste
1 tsp. **Paprika**

Blend processed cheese and cream cheese together in mixing bowl. Add garlic powder, lemon juice and red pepper and blend until fluffy. Place in refrigerator for about 1 hour. When firm, remove and roll into a log shape. Sprinkle paprika over log and refrigerate again until ready to serve with your favorite tortilla chips.

Havasu Hot Artichoke Dip

1 can (14 oz.) **Artichoke Hearts**, well drained and chopped
1 cup **Mayonnaise**
1 cup gratead **Parmesan Cheese**
1 cup shredded **Mozzarella Cheese**
Garlic Powder, to taste

Combine all ingredients and mix well. Spoon into a lightly greased casserole dish and bake at 350 degrees for 20 minutes. Serve with tortilla chips or your favorite crackers.

Beef Dip

1 lb. **Ground Beef**
Garlic Powder, to taste
1 can (15 oz.) **Refried Beans**
1 lb. **Longhorn Cheese**, shredded
1/2 lb. **Jack Cheese**, shredded
1 jar (16 oz.) **Salsa**, mild, chunky style
1 can (4 oz.) diced **Green Chiles**

Sauté beef in large saucepan until brown. Drain and sprinkle with garlic powder to taste. Combine with balance of ingredients in a crockpot and cook on low until mixture forms a saucy dip (four to six hours).

Mule Train Meatballs

1 1/2 lbs. **Ground Beef**
1/2 cup **Quick-Cooking Oatmeal**
1/2 cup **Milk**
1 **Egg,** slightly beaten
1/4 cup minced **Onion**
2 tbsp. chopped **Parsley**
1 tsp. **Salt**
1/8 tsp. **Pepper**
1 cup **Grape Jelly**
1 cup **Catsup**
2 tbsp. **Dry Mustard**
2 tbsp. **Worcestershire Sauce**

Add beef, oatmeal, milk, egg, onion, parsley, salt and pepper to medium bowl and blend well. Shape into 1-inch balls and brown in a large skillet, draining fat when done. Set aside.

In a separate pan, add remaining ingredients and stir over medium heat until jelly melts and mixture begins to boil. Pour jelly mixture over meatballs and simmer for 20 minutes.

Serve warm. Makes 3 dozen bite-size meatballs.

Prospector's Pepper Dip

1 pkg. (12 oz.) **Cream Cheese,** softened
1 can (15 oz.) **Chili, without beans**
8 oz. **Monterey Jack Cheese with Jalapeño Peppers**

Spread cream cheese in the bottom of a glass pie plate. Add chili on top of cream cheese, spreading evenly. Next, cut cheese into thin slices and arrange on top of the chili. Bake for approximately 30 minutes in 350 degree oven until edges bubble or in microwave on High for approximately 10 minutes.

Serve with your favorite tortilla chips. Perfect for hungry crowds!

Burrito Roll-ups

The nice part about this appetizer is you don't need a stove!
Make 'em, roll 'em up and enjoy!

1 pkg. (8 oz.) **Cream Cheese**, softened
1 can (4 oz.) diced **Green Chiles**
1 medium **Onion**, chopped
1 cup **Sour Cream**
Pepper, dash
Garlic Salt, dash
6 large **Flour Tortillas**

Combine all ingredients (except tortillas) in a large bowl. Mix until well blended. Spread a thin layer of mixture on each tortilla. Roll each tortilla tightly; then wrap in waxed paper. Store in the refrigerator until ready to serve. Slice into bite-size pieces. Serve with salsa for a zesty treat. Makes about 6 dozen roll-ups.

Southwestern Stuffed Mushrooms

3/4 lb. medium-size fresh **Mushrooms**
8 tbsp. melted **Butter**
1 can (6 oz.) **Crabmeat**, drained and flaked
2 **Eggs**, slightly beaten
6 tbsp. **Bread Crumbs**
2 tbsp. **Mayonnaise**
2 tbsp. chopped **Onion**
2 tbsp. chopped **Chives**
1 tbsp. **Lemon Juice**
1/8 tsp. **Ground Pepper**

Clean mushrooms and remove stems. Chop stems and set aside. Next, brush mushroom caps with melted butter and arrange upside down on lightly greased baking pan.

In a small bowl, combine remaining ingredients except 1 tablespoon of butter and 2 tablespoons bread crumbs. Add mushroom stems and blend well.

Fill each mushroom cap with stem mixture. Sprinkle with remaining butter and bread crumbs. Place in preheated 375 degree oven and bake for 15 minutes. Serve warm.

Rimrock Zucchini Frittatas

These frittatas can be prepared ahead of time and stored in the refrigerator.
Serve them at your next pot luck get-together and you'll be the hit of the party!

1 cup **Bisquick**
4-5 medium **Zucchini**, thinly sliced or grated
1/2 cup **Vegetable** or **Olive Oil**
4 **Eggs**, slightly beaten
1/2 cup chopped **Onion**
1/2 cup grated **Parmesan Cheese**
1 clove **Garlic**, chopped
2 tbsp. **Parsley**
1/2 tsp. **Salt**
1/2 tsp. **Oregano**
Ground Pepper, to taste

Preheat oven to 350 degrees (375 degrees for higher altitudes). Combine all ingredients in a medium size bowl and blend well. Spread mixture in a greased 13"×9"×2"pan. Bake for about 30 minutes, until the top is golden brown. Make sure mixture is set in the middle before removing from oven. Allow to cool for approximately 15 minutes. Cut into 1-inch squares and serve.

Colorado Beef Spread

1 pkg. (8 oz.) **Cream Cheese**, softened
2-3 **Scallions**, chopped
1 small jar **Chipped Beef**, diced
Cayenne Pepper, to taste

Mix all ingredients together in bowl. Shape into a ball, cover with plastic wrap and place in refrigerator overnight. When ready to serve, remove and allow to stand at room temperature until softened. Serve with your favorite tortilla chips for a tasty snack.

Green Chile Guacamole

3 ripe **Avocados**
1/2 pint **Sour Cream***
1/2 cup **Diced Green Chiles**
1 clove **Garlic,** chopped
1 tsp. finely chopped **Onion**
1/4 cup diced **Tomato**
Salt, to taste

Peel, pit and mash avocados. In a medium bowl, combine remaining ingredients with mashed avocados. Blend until avocado mixture is smooth and creamy. Salt to taste. Place guacamole on bed of lettuce and serve cold with your favorite tortilla chips.

* You may substitute creamed cottage cheese for sour cream.

Glen Canyon Chicken Wings

*We make this recipe to take along to snack on
while watching the sunset at beautiful Lake Powell.*

1 lb. **Chicken Wings**
1 cup **Soy Sauce**
1 1/3 cups **Brown Sugar**
3/4 cup **Water**
1/4 tsp. **Garlic Powder**
Paprika, to taste

Pat chicken wings dry and place in a pan. Mix together soy sauce, brown sugar, water, and garlic powder. Add soy mixture to chicken, cover, and marinate in refrigerator overnight or for at least 8 hours. When ready to cook, pour off marinade and reserve. Bake chicken in a 350 degree oven for 1 hour. Baste with marinade while cooking. When done, sprinkle with paprika and serve with rice, pineapple rings or mandarin oranges for a festive presentation.

Zones of Life in the Grand Canyon

The elevations of the Grand Canyon range from 1,300 feet at the bottom to 7,400 feet at the rim. This variation accounts for several different life zones found at the Canyon. Each zone, defined by elevation, may overlap another. Each has distinguishable characteristics that help define its plant and wildlife. A difference in altitude of only a few feet can mean the difference of life or death to a migrating plant or animal.

For example, the temperature on the North Rim of the Grand Canyon averages around 35 degrees colder than the temperature at the bottom of the canyon. In the spring there could be deep snow on the rim, while flowers bloom in the desert heat below. In the summer, temperatures can climb well above 120 degrees in the shade at the bottom of the Canyon!

Snow rarely reaches the canyon floor; it just melts and evaporates on the way down. Only about 6 inches of rainfall reaches the bottom each year. In a record snowfall in 1931, the North Rim received over 17 feet of snow. The South Rim received only 8 feet that same year. And the canyon floor didn't receive a trace!

Included among the variety of trees in the canyon is the Piñon Pine. Piñon nuts, featured in several recipes in this cook book, were a staple in the native people's diet for centuries.

Beverages

Canyon Tomato Shake

1 cup **Cream**
2 cups **Tomato Juice**
4 **Celery Stalks**, grated
1/4 cup **Crushed Ice**
Pinch of **Salt**
Pinch of **Cayenne**
One drop of **Hot Sauce**

Chill cream and tomato juice. Combine all ingredients in a shaker or glass jar. Shake vigorously and pour over crushed ice. Serves 4.

Lemon Pear Nectar

This tastes great on a hot summer day!

2 cups **Cold Water**
Juice of 1/2 **Lemon**
2 tbsp. **Raisins**
1 can (16 oz.) **Pears**, drained

Blend all ingredients together in a large blender. Refrigerate for 2 hours and serve over ice. Serves 2.

Prospector's Cider

This cider will warm you up from the inside!

4 qts. **Apple Juice**
2 qts. **Cranberry Juice**
1 can (6 oz.) **Lemonade**, frozen
6 **Cinnamon Sticks**

Mix all ingredients and heat slowly over low heat for 2 hours. Serves 20.

Piñon Nut Milk

Especially good on hot cereals!

1/2 cup **Piñon Nuts**
2 cups **Water**
3 **Dates**
1 **Banana**
1/2 tsp. **Salt**

Using a blender, combine ingredients together. Can be used immediately or refrigerated for a nutritious and tasty drink.

Pioneer Lemon Tea

1 pkg. (2 oz.) **Lemon Flavor Tea Mix**
1 pkg. (2 oz.) **Mint Flavor Tea Mix**
4 cups **Cold Water**
1/2 tsp. **Cinnamon**
Ice Cubes

Dissolve instant tea mixes in water; add the cinnamon and serve over ice cubes in chilled glasses. Garnish each glass with a slice of lemon.

Hiker's Tea

This tea is great for sipping around the campfire after a hard day of hiking or sightseeing. Each person can decide for themselves how much brandy to put in their tea!

1 cup of **Hot Tea**
Brandy
3 tsp. **Honey**

Combine ingredients in cup, stir gently, and sit back and relax!

Settler's Egg Nog

6 **Eggs**, separated
1 cup **Granulated Sugar**
2 qts. **Light Cream**
3/4 cup **Cognac**
1/2 cup **Rum**
1/2 cup **Powdered Sugar**

Beat the egg yolks in a large bowl until thick. Then add the granulated sugar, beating until it becomes light. Next add the cream. Beat the mixture until it becomes condensed. Stir in the cognac and rum. Refrigerate, covered, for a minimum of 3 hours. One hour before serving, beat the egg whites until soft peaks form. Gently add the powdered sugar, blending after each addition. Fold in the egg yolk mixture. Cover and refrigerate until you're ready to serve.

Top with whipped cream and nutmeg. Serves 12.

Orange Surprise

2 cups **Orange Juice**
1/2 cup **Water**
1/2 cup **Evaporated Milk**
Pinch of **Salt**
2 tbsp. **Powdered Sugar**
1 tsp. **Almond Extract**
1/2 cup **Ice**, crushed
Orange Slices

Combine ingredients and mix vigorously. Pour into chilled tall glasses. Serve with straws and a slice of orange. Serves 3.

Hot Buttered Rum

You can freeze this mixture for future use on cold winter nights.
It's the perfect drink to sip while watching the stars.

1 cup **Vanilla Ice Cream**, softened
1/4 lb. **Butter**, softened
1/2 cup **Brown Sugar**
1 cup **Powdered Sugar**
1/4 tsp. **Nutmeg**
1/2 tsp. **Cinnamon**
1 jigger **Rum**
1 cup **Hot Water**

Blend the ice cream together with the butter, brown sugar, powdered sugar, nutmeg and cinnamon. To serve, place 2 tablespoonfuls of ice cream mixture in a mug and add rum and hot water.

Mexican Chocolate Milk

1 1/4 cups **Water**
1 tsp. **Sugar**
1 tsp. **Cinnamon**
Chocolate Milk

Combine 1/2 cup water, sugar and cinnamon. Boil for one minute. Add remaining 3/4 cup water. Pour into a 6-cup muffin pan and freeze. To serve, place 1 cinnamon ice cube in each cup of chocolate milk. The cube melts and adds its flavors to the drink.

Banana Float

You can use this drink as a dessert for all ages!

2 ripe **Bananas,** mashed
3 cups cold **Milk**
1 pkg. frozen **Strawberries,** thawed
1 tsp. **Honey**
1 tbsp. **Vanilla**
1 pint **Chocolate Ice Cream**

In a blender, thoroughly combine the bananas, milk, strawberries, honey, and vanilla. Add 1/2 of the chocolate ice cream and blend again just to combine. Pour into tall, chilled glasses and top each glass with a scoop of chocolate ice cream. Serves 4-6.

Citrus Cooler

3 **Tea Bags**
1 1/2 cups **Boiling Water**
1 cup **Sugar**
1/2 cup fresh **Lemon Juice**
1/2 cup fresh **Orange Juice**
1 bottle (28 oz.) **Ginger Ale,** chilled
1 tray **Ice Cubes**
Orange Slices

Place tea bags in a large bowl. Pour boiling water over tea bags. Let stand for 5 minutes. Remove tea bags. Add sugar and stir until completely dissolved. Pour lemon juice, orange juice and ginger ale into tea mixture and stir briskly. Place ice cubes in a 2-quart serving pitcher and add tea mixture.

Serve in chilled glasses garnished with orange slices. Serves 6.

Frozen Margaritas

1/2 cup **Triple Sec**
2 cups **Tequila**
2 qts. **Sweet and Sour Mix**
2 cups **Crushed Ice**
Margarita Salt
Fresh Limes

In a bowl, mix together the triple sec, tequila, sweet and sour mix and crushed ice and place in the freezer for 24 hours. About one hour before the party starts remove the mixture from the freezer and allow to thaw somewhat (you want a good, slushy consistency to the mix). Cut the limes into wedges and run each slice around the lip of the margarita glass. Dip the edge of each glass in the margarita salt, pour in the margarita mix and place the lime wedge on the rim. You're now ready to start your party! Serves 10-12.

Canyon Cappuccino

This makes a nice, relaxing after-dinner drink.

3 cups **Coffee**
3 cups **Half and Half**
1/2 cup **Dark Crème De Cacao**
1/4 cup **Rum**
1/4 cup **Brandy**

Combine all ingredients in a saucepan and heat. Serve piping hot! Serves 8.

Hot Desert Tea

3 cups **Boiling Water**
1/3 cup **Sugar**
3 **Tea Bags**
12 whole **Cloves**
1 stick **Cinnamon**
1 strip fresh **Orange Peel**
1/2 cup fresh **Orange Juice**
3 tbsp. **Lemon Juice**
Lemon Slices, studded with **Whole Cloves**

Pour boiling water over the sugar, tea bags, spices and orange peel. Steep for five minutes and then strain mixture. Stir in orange and lemon juices. Heat, but do not boil. Serve in cups garnished with lemon slices studded with whole cloves. Serves 4.

Chilly Date Malt

The dates bring a thick rich flavor to this malt.
Drink slowly, it lasts longer that way!

1 cup **Dates**, pitted and chopped
1 1/2 cups **Milk**, cold
1 pint **Vanilla Ice Cream**
1 tbsp. **Vanilla**
2 tbsp. **Malted Milk**

Put dates and 1/2 cup of milk in a blender and blend on High until mixture is smooth. Add the rest of the milk, ice cream, vanilla and malted milk and blend on low speed till fully mixed. Serve immediately in chilled glasses. Serves 4.

Arizona Sangria

1 bottle (750 ml) **Red Wine**
1 **Orange**, peeled and squeezed
1 **Lemon**, sliced
1 **Lime**, sliced
3 tbsp. **Brandy**
1 fresh **Peach**, sliced
1/2 cup fresh **Raspberries**
1 bottle (7 oz.) **Sparkling Water**

Pour the wine into a large glass pitcher. Peel the orange in a long spiral strip. Put the peel in the wine, with one end of the spiral curled over the spout of the pitcher. Squeeze the orange, and add the juice to the wine along with the lemon and lime slices and the brandy. Allow this to stand in the refrigerator for three hours. One hour before serving add the remaining fruit.

Before serving, add sparkling water. Pour Sangria into tall glasses half-filled with ice cubes. If desired, add additional fruit to glasses.

Hiking the Canyon

Bright Angel and Kaibab trails, the most popular trails in the canyon, are maintained by the National Park Service. Kaibab Trail begins near Yaki Point, which is about 4 miles from Grand Canyon Village. The Bright Angel Trail begins near the Bright Angel Lodge in Grand Canyon Village.

Indian Gardens, a delightful oasis, is about halfway down the Bright Angel Trail. From here, some hikers continue to the bottom, others hike to Lookout Point, and still others soak their feet in the refreshing spring water before returning to the Rim.

The Widforss Trail is a foot path which meanders along a huge side canyon called the Transept. This trail provides spectacular views of the canyon from the North Rim. Widforss Point is named after a Swedish artist, Gunnar Widforss, who made his living painting scenery in the western national parks.

It's very important to take the proper amount of food and water with you when you hike the canyon. Mistakes can be deadly. Each person hiking the Grand Canyon from river to rim is required to carry a minimum of one gallon of water. Your needs for food and water change with the seasons. Always check with park rangers to find out about local weather conditions.

Plan your meals ahead of time for your hiking and backpacking trips. Pack plenty of protein and carbohydrate snacks for quick energy on the trail. Many of the recipes in this section can be made days in advance and stored and packed for later use.

Trail Food

Roasted Pine Nuts

When you're on the trail, these nuts make a great snack! Kids of all ages will love these for in-between meal snacks. Be sure and save some for yourself!

2/3 stick **Butter**
1 lb. **Pine Nuts**
1 tbsp. **Salt**
1 tsp **Cinnamon**

Melt butter in large shallow baking pan. Add the nuts, salt and cinnamon. Bake at 300 degrees for 30 minutes, stirring nuts every 10 minutes. Remove the nuts from the oven and drain them on paper towels. When they have cooled, place in airtight plastic bags.

Hiker's Hot Chocolate

We pack this hot chocolate mix on all our camping trips.
It keeps well and tastes so sweet around a campfire!

1 box (25 oz.) **Nonfat Dry Milk Powder**
1 jar (6 oz.) **Powdered Nondairy Coffee Creamer**
1 lb. **Powdered Sugar**
1 can (16 oz.) **Pre-Sweetened Cocoa Powder**

Combine all ingredients thoroughly. Store in airtight plastic bags. To use, place 2 tablespoonsful in a cup of hot water.

Fruit Pemmican

2 cups **Raisins**
2 cups **Dried Dates**
1 cup **Nuts**
1 cup **Dry Cereal**
3 tbsp. **Honey**

Grind together all ingredients except the honey. Place mixture in a bowl and add honey a little at a time, mixing well, until moist enough to mold well and hold a shape. In a square pan or dish spread mixture to about 1 inch deep. Refrigerate for three hours, cut into bars and wrap in aluminum foil.

High Energy Bars

Try one of these on your next rest stop on the trail.
These bars are a great energy boost!

1/2 cup **Butter**, softened
3/4 cup **Brown Sugar**
1/2 cup **Quick-Cooking Rolled Oats**
1/2 cup **Whole Wheat Flour**, unsifted
1/2 cup **All-Purpose Flour**, unsifted
1/4 cup **Wheat Germ**
2 tsp. grated **Orange Rind**
2 **Eggs**
1 cup **Whole Almonds**, blanched
1/4 cup **Raisins**
1/4 cup **Coconut**, flaked
1/2 cup **Chocolate Bits**, semi-sweet

Cream butter with 1/2 cup brown sugar until smooth. Then blend in oats, flours, wheat germ and orange rind. Put mixture in a lightly greased 8-inch square pan. Next mix eggs, almonds, raisins, coconut, chocolate bits and 1/4 cup remaining brown sugar. Pour over the mixture in the pan and spread out evenly. Bake at 350 degrees for 35 minutes or until golden brown. Let cool, cut into a dozen bars and wrap each in aluminum foil.

Canyon Trail Food

Freeze these bars and eat them on the trail later.

3 cups **Quick-Cooking Rolled Oats**
2 1/2 cups **Powdered Milk**
1 cup **Brown Sugar**
3 tbsp. **Water**
3 tbsp. **Honey**
1/2 pkg. **Flavored Gelatin**
1/4 cup chopped **Dried Apricots**

Mix the oatmeal, powdered milk and brown sugar together. Add 3 tablespoons water to the honey and bring to a boil in a large shallow pan. Dissolve the gelatin in the honey-water mix. Add the oatmeal mixture and blend well. Add water, a teaspoonful at a time, until the mixture is moist enough to mold. Make into bars and wrap in aluminum foil.

River Runner's Bars

*Each bar provides approximately 400 calories and will keep indefinitely;
just don't eat them while you're running the rapids!*

3 cups **Dry Cereal**, (oats, wheat germ, corn flakes, etc.)
2 1/2 cups **Powdered Milk**
1 cup **Granulated Sugar**, white or brown
1/4 tsp. **Salt**
3 tbsp. **Honey**
3 tbsp. **Water**
1/2 pkg. **Citrus-Flavored Gelatin**

Place dry ingredients in a mixing bowl and mix well. Combine the
honey and water in a pan and bring to a boil. Dissolve the gelatin in the
honey-water mixture. Add to dry ingredients and mix well. Add
additional water a teaspoonful at a time until the mixture is soft enough
to mold. Make into bars about 2 to 3 inches long and approximately 2
inches wide. Wrap each bar in aluminum foil.

Iron Bars

1/3 cup **Butter**, softened
1/2 cup **Sugar**
1/2 cup **Molasses**
1 **Egg**
1 1/4 cups **Whole Wheat Flour**
1/4 cup **Nonfat Dry Milk**
1/4 cup **Toasted Wheat Germ**
1 1/2 tsp. **Baking Powder**
1/2 tsp. **Baking Soda**
1/2 tsp. **Salt**
1/2 tsp. **Ginger**
1/2 cup **Milk**
1 cup **Quick-Cooking Rolled Oats**
1 cup chopped **Dark Raisins**
1/2 cup chopped **Golden Raisins**
1 cup sliced **Almonds**

Cream butter, sugar, molasses and egg together. Combine whole wheat
flour, nonfat dry milk, wheat germ, baking powder, baking soda, salt
and ginger and mix lightly. Blend into creamed mixture alternately with

liquid milk. Stir in oats, raisins, and half of the almonds. Turn into a greased 9 × 12 baking pan and spread evenly. Sprinkle with remaining half cup of almonds. Bake in a 350 degree oven about 30 minutes. Let cool in pan and then cut into bars.

Peanut Chocolate Bars

1/2 cup **Peanut Butter**, chunky style
1/2 cup **Honey**
1/2 cup **Dry Milk Powder**
1 pkg. (8 oz.) **Semi-Sweet Chocolate**, melted

Heat peanut butter in a double boiler until it is a thick soup. Stir in the honey and then the dry milk. Mix well and remove from heat. Pour into cupcake papers and refrigerate. When cool, coat with semi-sweet or dipping chocolate.

Date Bars

1/2 cup **Date Sugar**
1 1/4 cups **Quick-Cooking Rolled Oats**
1 cup **Whole Wheat Flour**
1/2 tsp. **Salt**
1/2 cup **Corn Oil**
1 cup **Hot Water**
2 tbsp. **Lemon Juice**
1 lb. **Dates**, diced
1/2 cup chopped **Walnuts**

Combine the date sugar, oats, whole wheat flour, salt and corn oil. Make a date butter filling by mixing the water with the lemon juice and the dates in a saucepan and simmering until the mixture is smooth. Using a 9 × 11 inch baking dish, press half of the dry mixture into the dish. Spread the warm date butter over the dry mixture about 1/2 inch thick. Sprinkle nuts over the date filling, lightly pressing them into the filling. Press remainder of dry mixture evenly on top. Bake in a 350 degree oven for 15 minutes. Let cool and cut into bars. For hiking or camping, wrap the bars in aluminum foil.

Prospectors, Burros and Mules

At one time, there were 83 mining claims in the Grand Canyon. Elements such as asbestos, copper, silver, platinum and lead were extracted. It was soon discovered that the costs involved in transporting the ores out of the canyon made mining unprofitable. The only remaining signs of the eager prospectors are a few trash dumps.

Many miners abandoned their claims and their burros! The wild burros now roam the Canyon feeding on any vegetation they can find.

Today, many visitors enjoy the inner canyon while on muleback. Rides are very popular, thus reservations must be made well in advance. Mules are used because they are more sure-footed, stronger and not as likely to be "spooked" as a horse.

Sure-footed mules are also used as pack animals to carry supplies in and out of the Canyon.

Adventurers know the importance of a hearty breakfast to start their day! The tasty breakfasts in this next section of The *Grand Canyon Cook Book* are designed to get you up and out the door!

Breakfasts

Mexican Eggs

1/4 cup **Corn Oil**
1/2 cup diced **Green Bell Pepper**
1/2 cup diced **Onion**
1 cup fresh chopped **Tomato**
1 tsp. **Black Pepper**
1 can (4 oz.) diced **Green Chiles**
6 **Eggs**
1/2 cup grated **Cheddar Cheese**
1/2 cup grated **Monterey Jack Cheese**
Salsa
Corn Tortillas

In a baking dish, mix together the first six ingredients. Microwave on High, covered, for 5 minutes. Stir mixture and then break eggs over the top. Pierce each yolk and egg white at least once. Combine cheeses and sprinkle on top. Cover dish, return to microwave and cook on High for 3 to 5 minutes or until the eggs are done. Let stand for 3 minutes. Serve with warm corn tortillas and a side of salsa. Serves 4.

Dirty Devil Eggs

1/2 cup chopped **Onion**
1/4 cup chopped **Green Pepper**
2 tbsp. **Butter**
1 jar (8 oz.) **Cheese Whiz®**
4 **Hard-Boiled Eggs**, sliced or chopped
4 **English Muffins**, split

Sauté onion and green pepper in butter until onion becomes translucent. Add cheese and eggs to pan. When cheese mixture is well heated, spoon over toasted muffins. Serves 4.

Canyon Huevos Rancheros

This is a popular breakfast dish throughout the Southwest.
Tastes even better the day after a long day of hiking.

1/2 cup **Vegetable Oil**
1/4 cup diced **Onion**
1/2 cup diced **Green Bell Pepper**
1 can (28 oz.) **Whole Tomatoes**, drained
1 can (4 oz.) **Green Chiles**, drained
1/4 tsp. **Ground Pepper**
6 **Eggs**
1 cup shredded **Cheddar Cheese**
6 **Corn Tortillas**, warmed
Salsa

In a 13 × 9 × 2 glass baking dish, combine oil, onion and green pepper. Microwave on High 5-7 minutes, stirring occasionally until onion is translucent and green pepper is tender. Add tomatoes to dish, mashing with fork. Stir in green chiles and ground pepper. Cover with plastic wrap and cook on high for 5 minutes, stirring after 3 minutes. Break eggs over tomato mixture along edge of dish. With a toothpick, pierce each egg yolk twice and each egg white 3 times.

Cover dish with plastic wrap and microwave an additional 4 to 7 minutes, or until eggs are done to taste. Sprinkle with cheese. Cover and allow to stand 5 minutes. Serve over warmed corn tortillas and top with your favorite salsa.

Hopi Hotcakes

Using the blue cornmeal will give a beautiful blueish tint to your hotcakes.
Add blueberries for a matching color and memorable flavor.

1/3 cup **Quick-Cooking Rolled Oats**
1/3 cup **Flour**
1/3 cup **Blue Cornmeal**
2 tbsp. **Brown Sugar**
1 tsp. **Baking Powder**
1/2 tsp. **Baking Soda**
1/4 tsp. **Salt**, optional
2 large **Eggs**, separated
1 cup **Buttermilk**

Combine all dry ingredients together in large mixing bowl. In a separate bowl, slightly beat egg yolks. Slowly add buttermilk to egg yolks. Next, add egg mixture to dry ingredients, stirring until moist. Beat egg whites until stiff; then fold into batter.

Prepare large skillet or griddle by brushing with vegetable oil. Heat. Spoon batter onto griddle (about 1/2 cup per hotcake). Turn when bubbles form on surface. Serve with blueberries, applesauce, syrup, preserves or any of your favorite condiments.

Kaibab Casserole

1 lb. **Cheddar Cheese**, grated
1 lb. **Monterey Jack Cheese**, grated
2 cans (4 oz. ea.) **Diced Green Chiles**, drained
4 **Eggs**, separated
1 can (8 oz.) **Evaporated Milk**
1 tbsp. **Flour**
1/2 tsp. **Salt**
1/2 tsp. **Pepper**
2 medium **Tomatoes**, sliced

In a large bowl combine cheeses and chiles. Pour into a well-buttered, shallow 2-quart casserole dish. Beat egg whites until they form peaks. In another bowl, combine egg yolks, milk, flour, salt and pepper. Mix well with a rubber spatula. Gently fold the whites into the egg yolk mixture. Use a fork to poke holes in the top of the cheese mixture, then pour egg mixture evenly over all. Bake for 30 minutes in a 350 degree oven. Place the tomato slices on top and bake for an additional 30 minutes. Serves 4 to 6.

Ranger Egg Patties

A ranger we met on the South Rim shared this recipe for breakfast.
It will stick with you all morning!

4 **Eggs,** well-beaten
1 cup **Milk**
1 pinch **Coriander**
Salt, to taste
Pepper, to taste
1/2 cup **Cooked Rice**
1 tbsp. **Cheddar Cheese,** grated

Combine beaten eggs, milk and seasonings until well blended. Fold rice and cheese into mixture. Mix thoroughly. Form mixture into round patties in hot skillet and cook until eggs are done. Serves 3. Serve with your favorite salsa on the side.

Prospector's Waffles

2 **Eggs,** separated
1 pt. **Sour Cream**
1 tsp. **Baking Soda**
3 cups **Flour**
1 tbsp. **Cornmeal,** white or yellow
1/2 tsp. **Salt**

Beat egg yolks and mix with sour cream. Add baking soda, flour, cornmeal and salt. Fold in stiffly beaten egg whites. Pour mixture into waffle iron until it is almost full; bake on hot until golden brown. Serve with your favorite condiments such as honey, syrup, butter or preserves. Serves 4.

Canyon Quiche

1 (9-inch) **Deep Dish Pie Shell**
1/2 lb. **Hot Sausage**
1/4 cup **Onion**, diced
3/4 cup grated **Swiss Cheese**
3/4 cup grated **Jalapeño Cheese**
1/4 cup chopped **Mushrooms**
4 **Eggs**
1 1/4 cups **Buttermilk**
1/2 tsp. **Salt**

Pre-bake pie shell at 350° for 5 minutes. Sauté sausage and onion together until sausage is done. Drain well. When cool, crumble sausage and sprinkle with onions, cheeses and mushrooms onto bottom of pie shell. Beat together eggs, buttermilk and salt. Pour egg mixture over sausage mixture. Bake at 375° for 30-40 minutes or until knife inserted near center comes out clean. Cool slightly before serving. Serves 6.

Miner's Griddle Cakes

1/2 cup **Flour**
1 tsp. **Baking Powder**
1/2 tsp. **Salt**
2 **Eggs**, well-beaten
1 cup **Milk**
2 cups **Cooked Rice**
2 tbsp. **Vegetable Oil**

Combine flour, baking powder and salt. Beat eggs with milk and add to flour mixture. Add rice and oil and mix thoroughly. Spoon onto hot griddle and cook until golden brown. Turn and repeat. When done, remove and serve hot with your favorite condiments such as syrup, honey, butter or preserves. Serves 4.

Breakfast Fry Bread Taco

*This recipe comes from John Kingsmore, Executive Chef
at the El Tovar Hotel at the Grand Canyon.*

3/4 cup **Milk**
1/4 cup **Sugar**
2 tsp. **Salt**
4 1/2 tbsp. **Shortening**
3/4 cup **Warm Water**
1 pkg. **Yeast**
2 1/4 cups **All-Purpose Flour**
2 1/4 cups **Flour,** additional

In a saucepan, bring milk, sugar, salt and shortening to a simmer. Remove from heat and cool to room temperature. Place warm water and yeast in a bowl and add milk mixture. Add flour and mix until smooth. If sticky, add additional flour. On bread board, work dough until smooth and elastic. Cover and let rise until double in volume. Punch down and divide into six equal pieces. Roll into circles and reserve.

Topping:

12 **Eggs**
6 oz. **Roasted Julienne Peppers**
12 oz. **Pulled Smoked Chicken Meat**
6 oz. **Black Beans,** cooked
12 oz. grated **Jalapeño Jack Cheese**

In a heavy pan, heat oil and fry dough circle. Arrange circles on a shallow baking pan. In another pan, sauté roast peppers, chicken and black beans. Add eggs and cook until all are just bound. Place egg mixture on top of dough rings and top with cheese. Flash under broiler to melt cheese and then cut into quarters. Serve with your other favorite breakfast dishes. Enjoy!

Major John Wesley Powell

In 1869, Major John Wesley Powell, a one-armed Civil War veteran, set out to travel the entire length of the Grand Canyon with nine other men. Powell, a teacher, scientist and geologist, chronicled his journey from Green River, Wyoming down the Colorado River.

Powell named his Chicago-built boats for the Colorado River expedition; Emma Dean, (after his wife), Maid of the Canyon, Kitty Clyde's Sister and No Name.

On June 9, the expedition lost the boat, No Name, as it crashed into large boulders during a run on angry rapids. Then, on June 16, a windy day helped to start a fire that ravaged the camp. The men lost their clothes, bedding and cooking utensils.

So powerful were some of the rapids on the Colorado that Major Powell and his men had to carry the boats around them. Despite the loss of four men, the incredibly powerful rapids and few supplies, Powell and five men safely emerged from the Grand Canyon with two boats at Grand Wash on the Nevada border near Pierce Ferry, Arizona on August 29, 1869.

The Colorado River today is not the same rough river that Major John Wesley Powell and his men knew! Now the many tributaries which comprise the Colorado River system are being used to supply water to our western states.

Soups and Salads

Spicy Spanish Soup

1 tbsp. **Olive Oil**
1 cup chopped **Onion**
1 **Celery Stalk**, diced
1/2 cup chopped **Jalapeños**
2 lbs. **Tomatoes**, peeled, seeded and chopped
1/2 cup chopped **Carrots**
1 tbsp. **Red Chile Powder**
1 tsp. **Sugar**
1 tbsp. **Flour**
4 cups **Chicken Broth**
1/4 cup shredded **Monterey Jack Cheese**

In a large saucepan heat the oil and sauté the onions, celery and jalapeños. Add the tomatoes, carrots, red chile powder and sugar. Stir the mixture until the moisture has evaporated and mixture has thickened. This should take about 15 to 20 minutes. Next, whisk in the flour and cook for 3 minutes stirring continuously. Add the chicken broth and let simmer for 30 minutes.

Pour into serving bowls, garnish with cheese and serve. Serves 4 to 6.

Indian Sunflower Soup

This soup has a deep, rich, nutty flavor. It's a great appetizer, too!

3 **Scallions**, washed and sliced
2 cups **Sunflower Seeds**, shelled
6 cups **Water**
2 pkgs. **Instant Chicken Broth**
1 tsp. **Salt**

Combine all ingredients in a large 4-quart pot. Simmer for 45 minutes, stirring every 5 minutes. Serves 6.

Arizona Split-Pea Soup

3 lbs. **Split Peas**
1 gal. **Chicken Stock**
1 lb. **Ham**, diced
1 small **Onion**, diced
4 **Carrots**, diced
4 cloves **Garlic**, minced
1 cup **Heavy Cream**
1 cup **Sherry**
1 tsp. **Salt**
1 tsp. **Cayenne Pepper**
1 tsp. **Cumin**, ground

Rinse and clean the split peas. Place the peas and chicken stock in large soup pot on high heat, bring to a boil, reduce heat and cook until peas are tender. Add ham, diced vegetables and garlic to peas. Let mixture simmer for 15 minutes. Add cream, sherry and seasoning and let simmer for 30 minutes.

Serve in mugs garnished with freshly ground black pepper. Serves 12.

Trout Bisque

1 can (12 oz.) **Cream of Celery Soup**
2 cups **Milk**
1 cup **Cheddar Cheese**
1/2 cup **Cooked Trout**
1/2 cup diced **Celery**
1/2 cup **Sherry**
1 tbsp. **Salt**

In a saucepan, combine celery soup and milk and bring to a simmer. Add the cheese, trout, celery, sherry and salt. Cover and let simmer for 15 minutes.

Serve with salad and French bread. Serves 4.

Jalapeño Cheese Soup

2 cups peeled and chopped **Tomatoes**
1 small **Onion**, diced
1 tbsp. chopped **Fresh Oregano**
2 **Jalapeños**, chopped
4 cups **Chicken Stock**
4 **Scallions**, chopped
2 tbsp. chopped **Fresh Cilantro**
1 cup grated **Jack Cheese**
1/2 cup grated **Cheddar Cheese**

In a blender, combine the tomatoes, onion, oregano and the jalapeño peppers until smooth. In a large pot blend the chicken stock and the tomato mixture. Bring to a boil and stir in the cilantro and the scallions.

Mix the cheeses together and then place 1/4 cup of cheese mixture in the bottom of each soup bowl. Pour the soup into each bowl over the cheese. Garnish with the remaining cheese and serve. Serves 4.

Yellow Squash Bisque

3 tbsp. **Margarine**
1 large **Onion**, chopped
4 medium **Yellow Squash**, chopped
1 1/2 cups **Water**
1 Chicken **Bouillon Cube**
1 tsp. dried **Basil**
1/2 tsp. dried **Thyme**
2/3 cup **Instant Milk Powder**
1/3 cup **Cool Water**
1/4 cup **Dry Sherry**
4 tbsp. **Sour Cream**
1/4 cup chopped fresh **Chives**
Ground Black Pepper

In a large pan melt margarine and add onions. Sauté until tender and then add yellow squash and cook until squash softens. Add water, bouillon cube, basil and thyme. Cover pan and let simmer for 15 minutes. Remove pan from heat and let the soup base cool to room temperature.

Purée the soup base in a blender until smooth. Mix the milk powder with 1/3 cup cool water until dissolved. Pour this mixture into the soup base. Pour the entire mixture back in the pan and cook over medium heat for 10 minutes.

Pour into soup bowls and garnish with sour cream, chives and black pepper. Serves 3-4.

Coronado Mushroom Soup

1 cup **Fresh Mushrooms**
4 cups **Water**
1 **Carrot**, diced
1 tsp. **Vinegar**
1 small **Onion**, chopped
4 medium **Red Potatoes**, cubed
1 tbsp. **Flour**
2 tsp. **Butter**
1 **Egg**, beaten
1 tsp. **Salt**
1 tbsp. **Pepper**

Wash and drain mushrooms, then cut them into small pieces. Put the 4 cups of water in a large kettle. Add mushroom pieces, carrots, vinegar and onion. Simmer for 45 minutes. Add potatoes and cook for 30 minutes on low heat. Brown the flour in the butter, stirring constantly to prevent burning. Add egg, salt and pepper to the flour mixture. Slowly add a cup of the soup liquid to the flour mixture and stir for 5 minutes. Add the flour mixture to the soup and bring to a slow boil. Serve with warm tortillas. Serves 4.

Vermillion Cliffs Chowder

1 qt. **Water**
6 slices **Bacon**
3 medium **Potatoes**, diced
1 can (12 oz.) **Creamed Corn**
3 **Scallions**, diced
3 **Carrots**, diced
1 can (8 oz.) **Evaporated Milk**
1 can (4 oz.) **Green Chiles**, diced

Bring water to a boil. Add bacon and potatoes. Let boil for 5 minutes. Add all other ingredients and lower heat to a simmer. Let simmer for 30 minutes.

Serve with cornbread and garnish with tortilla chips. Serves 4.

Cataract Canyon Carrot Salad

1 can (10 3/4 oz.) **Tomato Soup**
1/2 cup **Sugar**
1/2 cup **Vinegar**
1 lb. **Carrots**, sliced and parboiled
1 **Green Bell Pepper**, chopped
1 **Onion**, chopped

Heat soup, sugar and vinegar together. Add carrots, pepper and onion to sauce. Marinate overnight in refrigerator. Drain vegetables well and serve atop chilled lettuce.

Ambrosia Sunset Salad

1 cup **Pineapple Tidbits**, canned
1 can (6 oz.) **Mandarin Oranges**
1 cup **Marshmallows**, small
1 cup **Green Grapes**
1 cup **Coconut Flakes**
1 cup **Sour Cream**
2 tbsp. **Orange Juice**

Drain canned fruit. Mix all ingredients together and chill. Serve atop chilled lettuce leaves.

Southwestern Salad

3 cups **Cottage Cheese**
1/2 cup **Pineapple Juice**
1/2 tsp. **Salt**
1/2 tsp. **Chili Powder**
1/4 cup diced **Green Chiles**
6 **Pineapple Slices**

Mix all ingredients except pineapple slices. Place lettuce leaves on chilled salad plates. Place a slice of pineapple on each plate. Scoop cottage cheese mixture on each slice and serve with salad dressing or fruit salsa. Serves 6.

Hot Coleslaw

A friendly German couple we met at the Bright Angel Lodge gave us this recipe for zesty, hot coleslaw. This is a great conversation starter; try it for your next potluck dinner!

1 tbsp. **Butter**
1 **Egg,** well beaten
1/4 cup **Cider Vinegar** plus **Water** to make 2/3 cup liquid
1/2 cup **Cream,** sweet or sour
3 cups **Cabbage,** shredded

Heat butter, beaten egg and vinegar-water solution in two-quart pot. Add cream and stir until mixture coats spoon. Pour hot sauce over cabbage just before serving.

Spicy Spinach Salad

1 lb. **Spinach**
1/2 cup sliced **Green Onions**
10 **Mushrooms**, sliced
1/4 cup **Vegetable Oil**
2 tbsp. **Wine Vinegar**
1 tbsp. **Lemon Juice**
1/2 tsp. **Sugar**
1/4 tsp. **Dried Jalapeños**
1/8 cup diced **Green Chiles**
1/2 tsp. **Salt**
Pepper, to taste
1 **Hard-Cooked Egg**, chopped
1 tbsp. **Bacon**, cooked and crumbled

Wash spinach; discard the stems and pat dry with paper towels. Tear spinach into bite-size pieces in a medium-size bowl. Add onions and mushrooms to spinach, mix and chill. In a jar, combine oil, vinegar, lemon juice, sugar, jalapeños, chiles, salt and pepper. Shake vigorously. Toss dressing mix lightly with spinach, onions and mushrooms. Sprinkle egg and bacon over top and serve. Serves 4-6.

Tasty Tuna Salad

This can be either a salad or a sandwich!

1 1/2 cups **Cooked Macaroni**
1 cup **Cooked Peas**, drained
1 cup **Tuna**, drained
1/4 cup shredded **Cheddar Cheese**
1 **Egg**, hard-boiled and chopped
1/4 cup diced **Green Chiles**
2 tbsp. **Mayonnaise**
Mustard, to taste
Sugar, to taste
Salt and **Pepper**, to taste

Mix macaroni, peas, tuna, cheese, egg, chiles and mayonnaise together. Add mustard, sugar, salt and pepper to taste. Serve chilled atop a bed of lettuce.

For a delicious sandwich, spoon mixture onto sliced nine-grain bread.

Orange Pineapple Salad

1 1/2 cups **Cottage Cheese**
1/2 cup **Cool Whip**®
1 pkg. (3 oz.) **Orange Pineapple Jell-O**®
1 cup **Mandarin Oranges**, drained
1/2 cup **Pineapple Chunks**, drained
1 cup **Miniature Marshmallows**

Garnish:

1/4 cup **Coconut Flakes**

Mix all ingredients together, pour into a colorful serving bowl, chill and garnish with coconut flakes. Serves 4.

Territorial Taco Salad

1 lb. **Lean Ground Beef**
1/2 env. (1/4 cup) dry **Onion Soup Mix**
3/4 cup **Water**
1 **Head Lettuce**, torn
1 large **Tomato,** cut in wedges
1 small **Onion**, cut in rings
1/4 cup chopped **Green Bell Pepper**
1/2 cup sliced **Ripe Olives**
1 cup shredded **Monterey Jack** or **Cheddar Cheese**
1 pkg. (6 oz.) **Tortilla Chips**

In a large non-stick skillet, brown meat. Sprinkle with soup mix and stir in water. Simmer uncovered for approximately 10 minutes. In a salad bowl, toss remaining ingredients except tortilla chips. Drain meat and spoon atop salad mixture. Top with chips. Serves 4-6.

Ranch Coleslaw

4 cups finely shredded **Cabbage**
1/2 cup finely chopped **Green Bell Pepper**
1 tsp. **Salt**
1/8 tsp. **Pepper**
2 tbsp. **Granulated Sugar**
1 1/2 tsp. **Celery Seed**
2 tbsp. **Tarragon Vinegar**
1 tsp. **Mustard**
1/2 cup **Mayonnaise**

In a large salad bowl, mix all ingredients together. Toss well. Cover and allow to marinate overnight in refrigerator for full flavor. Serves 6.

Flagstaff Bean Salad

2 cans (15 oz. ea.) **Green Beans**
1 can (15 oz.) **petite Peas**
1/2 cup sliced **Stuffed Olives**
1 bunch **Celery,** diced
1 bunch **Scallions,** diced
4 **Carrots,** shredded
French Dressing, to taste
Salt, to taste
1/2 cup **Almonds**

Toss all ingredients together, holding back almonds and salt. Allow to chill overnight for full flavor. Just before serving, add salt to taste. Mix well. Top with almonds and serve. Serves 4-6.

Pueblo Carrot Salad

1 cup sliced **Carrots,** cooked
1 cup **Peas,** cooked
1/2 cup chopped **Cabbage**
1/2 cup chopped **Ripe Olives**
1 medium **Onion,** diced
2 cups **French Dressing**
Salt and **Pepper,** to taste
1/4 cup **Mayonnaise**
Paprika, to taste

Mix carrots and peas together and chill. Add cabbage, olives and onion and marinate in French dressing. Refrigerate for 30 minutes. Drain and season with salt and pepper. Place in lettuce cups. Garnish with mayonnaise and a dash of paprika.

The Kolb Brothers

At the turn of the century, many visitors came to the Grand Canyon, and often stayed at the El Tovar. Ellsworth and Emery Kolb capitalized on this development by setting up a photography business at the Grand Canyon in 1902. They built their studio on the edge of the Canyon, overlooking the Bright Angel Trail.

For many years the photographers took pictures of the mule riders as they began their journey down the Bright Angel Trail (the mule trains always stopped near the open window of their studio). Emery Kolb then ran the exposed film down the trail to Indian Gardens where there was a fresh supply of water. In an old shack that he and his brother had built, Emery developed the film. He then ran back up to the rim with the negatives to develop the prints in his studio so the trail riders would have them upon completing their journey.

As more and more mule trains used the trail, Emery found himself making the 4.5 mile trip twice a day! Even after the railroad began hauling water to service the Grand Canyon's growing needs, Emery continued to run his film down to Indian Gardens.

In 1974, when Emery Kolb was 93, he made a final nostalgic trip down the Colorado in one of the modern inflatable rafts.

The Kolb brothers studio still stands in its original spot at the beginning of the Bright Angel Trail.

Main Dishes

Grand Canyon Green Chile Burro

This makes a superb addition to your Southwestern brunch!

2 cups **Broth** or **Bouillon Cubes** with enough water to
  make 2 cups
1 tsp. **Oregano**
1 small **Onion**, chopped
2-3 cloves **Garlic**, pressed
1 can (16 oz.) **Whole Tomatoes**
2 cups cooked anddiced **Pork**
2 cups cooked and shredded **Beef**
2 cans (4 oz.) chopped **Green Chiles**
1 tsp. **Salt**, or to taste
2 tbsp. **Cornstarch**
Flour Tortillas, warmed

Place broth or bouillon and water in a large dutch oven. Add oregano,
onion, garlic and tomatoes. Cook until onion is tender. Add meat and
chiles and stir well. Cook at medium heat for 20 minutes. Make paste of
water and cornstarch and add to meat mixture. Cook slowly until thick.
Spoon onto warmed flour tortillas. Serves 4 to 6.

Amy's Chicken Enchiladas

Amy Snyder-Garvin is a lead server at the El Tovar Hotel.
She has always dreamed of having her recipes published. If you meet Amy at the
Grand Canyon, say you saw her recipe here. You'll make her day!

4 **Chicken Breasts**, bone in
3 tbsp. **Cooking Oil**
2 medium **Yellow Onions**, chopped
1 can (4 oz.) chopped **Green Chiles**
1/3 cup chopped **Fresh Cilantro Leaves**
1 tbsp. **Chili Powder**
1 1/2 tsp. **Ground Cumin**
1 tbsp. **Crushed Red Pepper**
2 cloves **Garlic**, minced
2 cans (10 3/4 oz. ea.) **Cream of Chicken Soup**
1 pt. **Sour Cream**
1 1/2 cups grated **Monterey Jack Cheese**
1 1/2 cups grated **Cheddar Cheese**

1 can (4 oz.) sliced **Black Olives**
1/2 cup chopped **Green Onions**
1 pkg. large **Flour Tortillas**

Boil chicken till tender. Cool and shred meat off the bone. In cooking oil, sauté chicken with next seven ingredients on medium heat until onions are translucent. If mixture begins to dry out, add a small amount of water.

Mix together cream of chicken soup, sour cream and 1/2 cup of each of the cheeses. Coat a (9 × 13 × 2) baking dish with non-stick cooking spray. Spread a thin layer of the cream mixture on bottom of dish.

Stuff tortillas with 2 heaping spoonfuls of chicken mixture and 3 level teaspoonfuls of cream mixture. Sprinkle olives, green onions and a handful of both cheeses on top. Roll up each tortilla and place in the pan. Evenly spread remaining cream mixture, olives, green onions and cheese over top. Cover with aluminum foil sprayed with cooking spray (spray side down). Bake at 350 degrees for 45 minutes. Let sit for 10 minutes before serving. Garnish enchiladas with shredded lettuce, chopped tomatoes and salsa. Serve with a side of refried beans topped with cheese, and guacamole. Serves 6.

River Casserole

1 medium **Onion**, chopped
1 cup chopped **Broccoli**
1 small **Green Bell Pepper**, chopped
1/4 lb. **Butter**
1 can (8 oz.) **Mushroom Soup**
1 cup grated **Cheddar Cheese**
1/2 cup grated **Monterey Jack Cheese**
2 cups **Cooked Rice**
1 can (4 oz.) diced **Green Chiles**

Sauté onion, pepper and broccoli in butter. Add the soup, cheeses and rice. Combine and place in a casserole dish. Bake at 350 degrees for 25 minutes. Serves 4.

Chile Relleno Casserole

1 can (1 1/2 lb.) **Whole Green Chiles**
1 lb. grated **Monterey Jack Cheese**
3 **Eggs**, beaten
1 tbsp. **Flour**
1 tsp. **Baking Powder**
3 tbsp. **Milk**
1 tsp. **Garlic Salt**
1 tsp. **Ground Cumin**
1 small **Red Bell Pepper**, diced

Remove all of the seeds from the chiles. Place a layer of chiles in an ungreased 9 × 13 baking dish. Then, place a layer of cheese followed by a layer of chiles, and continue layering until all the cheese and chiles have been used. Mix the eggs, flour, baking powder, milk, garlic salt, cumin and red pepper together and pour the mixture over the top. Bake in a pre-heated oven at 350 degrees for 25 minutes. Serve with salsa on the side. Serves 4.

Pork Chops with Rice

6 **Pork Chops**
2 tbsp. **Oil**
3 tsp. **Salt**
1 tsp. **Pepper**
1 cup **Rice**, uncooked
1 can (16 oz.) **Tomatoes**
2 cups **Water**
1/2 cup diced **Green Bell Peppers**
1/2 cup diced **Onions**
1/4 cup chopped **Black Olives**

Cook pork chops in oil until brown. Remove from the pan and season with salt and pepper. Wash rice and sauté it in the oil left in the pan, stirring constantly. Add the tomatoes, water, peppers, onions and black olives. Pour into a casserole dish and place the pork chops on top. Cover and bake in a pre-heated oven at 350 degrees for 40 minutes. Serve with salsa on the side. Serves 6.

Grand Canyon Chili

At Indian Gardens we met Frank Walberg, a veteran hiker in the canyon for many years, who shared this delicious chili recipe with us. Happy trails, Frank, wherever you are!

2 lbs. **Round Steak,** cubed
2 tbsp. **Oil**
1 large **Red Onion,** diced
1 tsp. **Salt**
1 tsp. **Chili Powder**
1 cup **Water**
1 tsp. **Dried Oregano**
1 tsp. **Ground Cumin**
1 can (16 oz.) **Stewed Tomatoes**
1 clove **Garlic,** minced
1 tsp. **Fresh Ground Pepper**
2 cans (16 oz. ea.) **Red Kidney Beans,** drained

In a large pot, brown meat in the oil. Add the rest of the ingredients except beans. Cover the pot and bring to boil. Reduce heat and simmer for 45 minutes, stirring occasionally. Skim off fat and add beans. Simmer for an additional 30 minutes. Serves 6.

Serving suggestion: Cornbread is perfect with this dish!

Fennel Crusted Trout

A favorite of diners at the El Tovar Hotel

1 cup **Dried Fennel Seed,** ground fine
1/3 cup **Flour**
1 tsp. **Salt**
1 tsp. **White Pepper**
4 (8 oz. ea.) **Boneless Trout**
1/2 cup **Egg Wash**

Mix together fennel, flour and seasonings. Brush trout with egg wash (beat yolk of 1 egg and add water to make 1/2 cup) and then coat with fennel mix. Sauté quickly in just enough oil to coat the bottom of the pan. Serve with lemon or melted butter and whole grain rice as a side dish.

Serving suggestion: Recommended wine selection with this dish is Sauvignon Blanc or Chardonnay.

Serves 4.

Indian Gardens Meat Loaf

Indian Gardens is truly an oasis for hikers! It is located a few miles below the rim,
and in the summer becomes a haven for tired hikers.
Be sure and linger awhile to enjoy the wildlife and
watch other hikers' expressions as they enter this beautiful hidden garden!

1 lb. **Ground Beef**
1/2 lb. **Ground Pork**
1/2 lb. **Ground Veal**
1/4 Onion, chopped
2 tbsp. diced **Celery**
2 tsp. **Salt**
1/4 tsp. **Pepper**
1/4 tsp. **Dry Mustard**
1/4 tsp. **Poultry Seasoning**
4 slices **Whole Wheat Bread**, cubed
1 cup **Milk**, warm
2 **Eggs**, beaten
1 tbsp. **Worcestershire Sauce**
1/2 cup **Dry Bread Crumbs**
1/2 cup **Boiling Water**

In a large bowl mix meats together. Add onion, celery and seasonings. Soak bread cubes in milk. Add eggs and Worcestershire sauce to the bread mixture and beat. Combine meat and egg mixtures and form into two loaves. Roll in bread crumbs and place in greased baking pan. Spread Brown Sugar Sauce over the top of each loaf. Place pan in larger pan. Pour about one inch of water in outside pan and bake uncovered for one hour in a 350 degree oven. Serves 8.

Brown Sugar Sauce

3 tbsp. **Brown Sugar**
1/4 cup **Catsup**
1/4 tsp. **Nutmeg**
1 tsp. **Dry Mustard**

Combine all ingredients in a small bowl.

Bright Angel Chicken

1 lb. **Vermicelli**
3 **Scallions**, diced
1 **Red Bell Pepper**, diced
1 **Chicken**, boiled, reserve 1 cup broth
1 can (4 oz.) **Mushroom Tops**
1 can (4 oz.) diced **Black Olives**
1/2 lb. grated **Cheddar Cheese**
1 cup **Bread Crumbs**

Bone and cube the chicken. Cook vermicelli in boiling water for 8 to 10 minutes. Drain and set aside in a large bowl. In a small amount of oil sauté the scallions and peppers in a small skillet. Add to the vermicelli and then add the chicken, mushrooms and olives. Combine all. Place chicken mixture in a greased 9 × 13 baking dish. Pour the chicken broth over all and top with the grated cheese. Sprinkle bread crumbs on top. Bake at 350 degrees for one hour.

Serves 4.

Piñon Nut Casserole

1 can (6 oz.) **Tuna**, packed in water
1 can (8 oz.) **Cream of Mushroom Soup**
1/2 cup chopped **Onion**
1 cup **Water**
1 tsp. **Pepper**
1/4 lb. chopped **Piñon Nuts**
1 cup diced **Celery**
1 tsp. **Salt**
1 can (16 oz.) **Chow Mein Noodles**

Drain the water from the tuna. Mix the tuna with the balance of the ingredients except for 1/2 of the noodles. Place in a large casserole dish and bake at 325 degrees for one hour.

Serve in individual bowls garnished with remaining noodles. Serves 4.

Colorado River Chili

*Running the Colorado River through the Grand Canyon is one of
the most exciting trips you can take. The guides feed you gourmet meals,
tell you stories, get you soaking wet in waterfights,
guide you through the raging rapids and bring you back in one piece!*

3 tsp. **Lemon Juice**
2 lbs. **Ground Turkey**
1 clove **Garlic**, chopped
1 small **Onion**, chopped
1 cup chopped **Green Bell Pepper**
2 cans (15 oz. ea.) **Stewed Tomatoes**
1 can (6 oz.) **Tomato Paste**
1 cup **Red Kidney Beans**, cooked
1 can (15 oz.) **Corn**
2 tsp. **Ground Pepper**
1 tsp. **Chili Pepper**
1/4 cup **Salsa**

Put lemon juice in a large non-stick frying pan, and add the turkey, garlic,
onion and green pepper. Cook until turkey is browned. Add and combine
the remaining ingredients and simmer for 30 minutes. Serves 4.

Bright Angel Lasagne

1 1/2 lbs. **Ground Beef**
1/2 lb. **Ground Italian Sausage**
1 **Onion**, chopped
1 can (6 oz.) **Tomato Paste**
1 can (8 oz.) **Tomato Sauce**
1 can (16 oz.) **Whole Tomatoes** (reserve juice)
1 tbsp. **Dried Oregano**
1 clove **Garlic**, minced
1 tsp. **Salt**
1 tsp. **Pepper**
3/4 lb. **Ricotta Cheese**
1 lb. **Mozzarella Cheese**, shredded
1 can (8 oz.) **Parmesan Cheese**
12 **Wide Lasagne Noodles**, cooked
1 cup chopped **Black Olives**

First brown the beef and sausage with the onion. Pour off the grease. Add tomato paste, tomato sauce, whole tomatoes, oregano, garlic, salt and pepper. Simmer mixture for one hour. Place 3 of the cooked lasagne noodles in the bottom of a 9 × 13 baking pan. Spread a layer of the meat sauce to cover noodles and then spread layers of ricotta, Parmesan and mozzarella cheeses. Layer more noodles, sauce and cheeses until you've reached the top of the dish. Add the juice from the can of whole tomatoes that you saved earlier. Top with a sprinkle of mozzarella cheese. Bake in a 350 degree oven for 45 minutes. Allow to cool 10 minutes before cutting into servings.

Serve with black olives sprinkled on top. Serves 4-6.

Western Broiled Steak

1 tsp. **Salt**
1/4 tsp. **Pepper**
1/4 tsp. **Garlic Powder**
1 (3 lb.) **Flank Steak**
2 tbsp. melted **Butter**

Mix the salt, pepper and garlic powder. Rub mixture on both sides of the steak. Brush steak with the melted butter. Let stand for one hour.

Heat the broiler and rack for 5 minutes. Broil the flank steak on the rack for about 5 minutes on each side. Remove to a warm plate. Let cool for about 3 minutes; then cut (against the grain) into serving size pieces. Serve with Angel Sauce on the side. Serves 6.

Angel Sauce

2 tbsp. **Tarragon Vinegar**
1/2 tsp. **Dried Tarragon**
1/2 cup **Mayonnaise**
1 **Egg Yolk**
Salt and **Pepper**, to taste

Combine the vinegar, tarragon, mayonnaise and egg yolk in the top of a double boiler. Place over hot, but not boiling water. Allow mixture to warm, beating with wire whisk until thickened. Season to taste with salt and pepper.

Pasta Pie

6 oz. **Vermicelli**
2 **Eggs**, beaten
1/4 cup grated **Parmesan Cheese**
2 tbsp. **Margarine**
1/2 cup chopped **Green Bell Pepper**
1/2 cup chopped **Onion**
1 cup **Sour Cream**
1 lb. **Italian Sausage**
1 can (6 oz.) **Tomato Paste**
1 cup **Water**
4 oz. grated **Mozzarella Cheese**

Break pasta in half and cook according to package directions. Drain pasta while it's still warm and mix with the eggs and Parmesan cheese. Place this mixture in a greased deep dish pie plate. Use a spoon to create a crust around the sides. In a small frying pan, melt the margarine and add the pepper and onion. Sauté until the onion is translucent. Add the sour cream and spoon mixture over the pasta. Cook the sausage in a non-stick frying pan and then drain excess grease. Add the tomato paste and water to the sausage. Mix well and let simmer for 10 minutes. Pour over the top of the sour cream mixture. Bake in a 350 degree oven for 25 minutes. Sprinkle the mozzarella over the top and continue baking for 10 minutes, or until the cheese has fully melted. Serve hot with garlic bread sticks. Serves 4.

Mexican Meat Loaf

2 lb. lean **Ground Beef**
1 tbsp. **Chili Powder**
1 tsp. **Salt**
1 tsp. **Ground Cumin**
1 medium **Onion**, chopped
1/2 cup **Soft Bread Crumbs**
1/4 cup sliced **Black Olives**
1 **Egg**, slightly beaten
1 can (8 oz.) **Tomato Sauce**
2 tbsp. grated **Cheddar Cheese**

Mix all ingredients except cheese together. Place in a 9-inch round casserole dish. Bake in a 350 degree oven for 45 minutes. Add the cheese to the top of the loaf and bake an additional 30 minutes. Serve with salsa on the side. Serves 4 to 6.

Cowboy Chili Rice

1 lb. lean **Ground Beef**
1/2 cup chopped **Onion**
1 tbsp. **Chili Powder**
1/2 tsp. **Dry Mustard**
1 pkg. (10 oz.) frozen **Corn**
1 cup diced **Green Bell Pepper**
1 can (15 oz.) **Tomato Sauce**
1 can (4 oz.) diced **Green Chiles**
1/2 cup **Water**
1 cup **Quick-Cooking Rice**
1/2 cup **Cheddar Cheese**

First brown the ground beef and onions in a large skillet. Drain excess liquid and add spices, corn, peppers, tomato sauce, chiles and water. Cover and bring to a full boil, stirring mixture constantly for 5 minutes. Stir in the rice and reduce heat. Sprinkle cheese on top, cover and let simmer for 5 minutes.

Serve with cornbread and butter. Serves 4.

Two Hour Chili

1 lb. **Ground Beef**
2 cups **Water**
1 can (16 oz.) chopped **Tomatoes**
1 large **Onion**, diced
1 clove **Garlic**, minced
3 stalks **Celery**, diced
1 **Green Bell Pepper**, chopped
2 **Bay Leaves**
1 tbsp. **Dried Parsley**
2 tsp. **Salt**
2 tbsp. **Sugar**
1 tbsp. **Chili Powder**
1 tsp. **Ground Cumin**
2 cans (16 oz. ea.) **Red Kidney Beans**

In a non-stick frying pan, brown the ground beef and then drain thoroughly. In a large stew pot combine all ingredients except beans. Cook on medium heat for 1 1/2 hours. Add beans and cook for an additional 30 minutes. This chili must be cooked for exactly two hours, no more, no less. Otherwise, you have to change the name! Serves 4 hungry people.

Big Turkey Casserole

1 lb. **Ground Turkey**
1/4 cup chopped **Onion**
1 can (15 oz.) **Tomato Sauce**
1 tbsp. **Garlic Salt**
1 tsp. **Basil Leaves**
1 tsp. **Dried Oregano Leaves**
1/2 cup grated **Romano Cheese**
1 1/2 cups **Lowfat Cottage Cheese**
1 **Egg**
1 lb. **Zucchini**
2 tbsp. **Flour**
1 cup shredded **Mozzarella Cheese**

First cook the ground turkey and onion in large skillet until the meat is brown. Drain excess liquid. Add tomato sauce and spices to the meat mixture. Bring to a boil. Simmer on low heat for 10 minutes.

Cut the zucchini into 1/4" strips. Mix together the Romano cheese, cottage cheese and the egg. Coat a 9 × 9 baking pan with vegetable cooking spray. Layer 1/2 of the zucchini, flour (sprinkle), cottage cheese mixture and meat sauce. Top with the mozzarella cheese, then repeat with the balance of ingredients topping again with the mozzarella. Bake uncovered for 45 minutes in a 350 degree oven. Let stand for 10 minutes before serving. Serves 4.

Chicken Paprika

4 **Chicken Breast Halves**
2/3 cup grated **Parmesan Cheese**
4 large **Celery Stalks**, chopped
4 small **Tomatoes**, chopped
1 tsp. **Salt**
1 tsp. **Pepper**
1 tbsp. chopped fresh **Tarragon**
2 cups **Heavy Cream**
1 tbsp. **Paprika**

Place chicken breasts in a large baking dish. Top with half of the Parmesan cheese. Add celery and tomatoes. Sprinkle with salt, pepper and tarragon. Pour the cream over all and top with the remaining cheese. Then sprinkle with paprika. Bake in a preheated oven at 350 degrees for 50 minutes. Serve over noodles. Serves 4.

Corn Bacon Bake

1 cup **Rice**, uncooked
1 tsp. **Salt**
1 tsp. **Pepper**
1 can (8 oz.) **Corn**
2 cans (8 oz. ea.) **Tomato Sauce**
1 cup **Water**
1/2 cup chopped **Red Bell Pepper**
1/2 cup chopped **Onion**
2 lbs. lean **Ground Beef**, uncooked
8 slices **Bacon**, lean

Start by spreading the rice in the bottom of a greased shallow casserole dish. Add a pinch of salt and pepper. Then spread a layer of corn. In a small bowl, mix one can of tomato sauce with 4 oz. of water. Pour over corn layer. Spread the pepper and onion over the tomato sauce layer. Crumble the uncooked ground beef and spread over the peppers and onions. Mix the other can of tomato sauce with 4 oz. water and pour over the meat layer. Arrange the bacon slices on top. Cover and bake in a preheated oven at 375 degrees for one hour. Uncover and continue to bake until the bacon is brown. Serves 6.

Tortilla Chicken

1 can (10 oz.) **Cream of Mushroom Soup**
1 can (10 oz.) **Cream of Chicken Soup**
1 can (8 oz.) **Evaporated Milk**
1 can (4 oz.) diced **Green Chiles**
1/2 cup pitted and diced **Black Olives**
1 bag (12 oz.) **Tortilla Chips**, crumbled
4 cooked **Chicken Breasts**, boned, skinned and diced
1/2 cup grated **Cheddar Cheese**
1/2 cup grated **Monterey Jack Cheese**

Blend the soups and milk together and add the green chiles and black olives. Place half of the tortilla chips in a large casserole dish. Place chicken on top of the tortilla chips. Pour the soup mixture over the chicken, and spread the other half of the chips on top. Combine cheeses and sprinkle over the chips. Bake in a preheated oven at 350 degrees for 30 to 40 minutes or until the cheeses are bubbly. Serves 4.

Tequila Chicken Special

*Served with margaritas and black beans on the side,
this makes for a colorful and tasty meal!*

2 tbsp. **Olive Oil**
1 clove **Garlic,** minced
1 **Green Onion**, chopped
2 **Anaheim Chile Peppers**, chopped
4 boneless **Chicken Breasts** (skin removed)
1 tsp. **Salt**
1 tsp. **Pepper**
1/2 cup **Tequila**
1/2 cup **Lime Juice**
1 tbsp. **Dried Rosemary**
2 tbsp. **Butter**

In a non-stick frying pan, heat one tablespoon of olive oil (medium heat). Add garlic, peppers and onion and sauté until the garlic is soft. Remove the vegetables from the pan.

Sprinkle the chicken with salt and pepper. Add the remaining oil to the frying pan and brown the chicken for about three minutes on each side. Add the tequila, lime juice, rosemary and sautéed vegetables. Cover and simmer for five minutes, or until the chicken is just done. Coat the chicken with butter, let simmer for another minute and serve. Serves 4.

Camels in the Canyon

In 1857, Lieutenant Edward F. Beale was chosen by the War Department to explore the Southwestern desert. Beale had an idea to use camels on the trip. He purchased 34 camels and hired Arab drivers from Tunis, Egypt and Smyrna. The camels were shipped to Texas and were herded to Fort Defiance, New Mexico Territory. The trip proved to be too much for the camel drivers and all but one of them quit. The remaining driver, Hadji Ali, became known to Americans as "Hi Jolly."

When the camels first reached the Grand Canyon, they proved effective. They could carry as much as 1,000 pounds of gear, needed no shoes, and could cross over jagged lava rock that other animals could not. Lt. Beale's report was favorable and predicted that all continental mail routes would soon be utilizing the camel.

The military asked Congress for money to purchase more camels. However, the camels were quite troublesome. They smelled bad, were quite disagreeable, and horses and mules would stampede at the mere sight or scent of them. Additionally, the mule skinners were unable to successfully secure supplies to the camels' backs.

When the Civil War broke out the Army forgot about the camels. After the war they simply turned them loose to fend for themselves. For many years the camels wandered across the Southwest, scaring people and frightening mules. In 1875, Nevada passed a law forbidding camels from running at large. Eventually hunters tracked down and destroyed them all.

Side Dishes

Hi Jolly Casserole

1/2 lb. **Black Beans**
3 cups **Water**
1 large **Onion**, chopped
3 **Scallions**, chopped
1 cup chopped **Green Bell Pepper**
1 clove **Garlic**, minced
1 tbsp. **Olive Oil**
1 **Bay Leaf**
1 tsp. **Salt**
1 tsp. **Pepper**

Rinse and pick over beans. Place in a large saucepan and cover with water. Bring to a boil and simmer for one hour.

Sauté onions, bell pepper and garlic in olive oil until tender. Combine sautéed ingredients and seasonings with beans and cook for one hour or until beans are tender and the liquid is thick. Remove bay leaf.

Serve over cooked brown rice and garnish with green onions. Serves 4 to 6.

Coconino Sweet Potatoes

1 can (1 lb. 13 oz.) **Sweet Potato Pieces**
2 tbsp. **Butter**
1 tsp. **Vanilla**
1/2 cup **Honey**
1/2 cup prepared **Mincemeat**
1 tsp. **Salt**
1/2 cup chopped **Piñon Nuts**

Drain the excess liquid from the sweet potatoes and reserve. Place potato pieces in a large saucepan. Add butter, vanilla and honey and simmer for 10 minutes. Add the mincemeat and salt. Simmer for 15 minutes, while basting occasionally with the liquid from the sweet potatoes. Sprinkle with nuts just before serving. Serves 4.

Ranch Style Beans

This recipe is shared by Frank Russell, a cowboy who has spent
many years traveling around Arizona and the Grand Canyon. Frank says that
these beans were one of his favorite meals when he was out on the trail.

3 cups **Pinto Beans**
2 cups **Tomato Puree**
1 medium **Onion**, chopped
1/2 cup chopped **Green Bell Pepper**
1 tbsp. **Honey**
1 tbsp. **Salt**
1 tsp. **Dried Oregano**
1 tsp. **Dried Sweet Basil**
1 **Bay Leaf**
1 clove **Garlic**, minced
1 tsp. **Ground Cumin**

Pick over beans and rinse in warm water. Place in a large pot and add hot water to cover. Let beans soak for 2 hours. Drain off water and again add enough hot water to cover the beans. Add tomato purée, onions, bell pepper, honey and seasonings. Bring to a boil, then let simmer for 2 hours. Remove bay leaf.

Serve with cornbread. Serves 4 to 6.

Bean Soufflé

3 cups **Kidney Beans**, cooked
1 1/2 cups grated **Cheddar Cheese**
Pinch of **Cayenne Pepper**
3 tbsp. **Catsup**
6 **Egg Yolks**, well beaten
6 **Egg Whites**, stiffly beaten

Combine all ingredients, adding the egg whites last, in a large greased baking dish. Bake in a 350 degree oven for one hour. Serve hot. Serves 4.

Spicy Green Chile Corn

For a spicier dish, try substituting jalapeños for the green chiles!

1 can (16 oz.) **Cream Style Corn**
2 tbsp. **Flour**
1 tbsp. **Sugar**
1 can (4 oz.) diced **Green Chiles**
2 **Eggs**, beaten lightly
2 tbsp. **Butter**

In a large bowl, combine corn, flour, sugar, and chiles. Add the two beaten eggs and stir. Pour mixture into a greased casserole dish. Dot butter on top and bake at 350 degrees for 30 minutes. Serves 4.

Mexican Grits

1 1/2 cups **Instant Grits**
2 tsp. **Salt**
3 **Eggs**, beaten
1 lb. **Longhorn Cheese,** shredded
1 tsp. **Pepper**
1 tsp. **Garlic Powder**
1 tsp. **Paprika**
2 drops **Hot Sauce**
1 can (4 oz.) chopped **Green Chiles**

Cook grits according to package instructions. Add the remaining ingredients and mix well. Place mixture in a 13 × 9 baking dish and bake at 300 degrees for 1 hour. Serve with meat dishes. Serves 4.

Green Chile Enchiladas

12 **Corn Tortillas**
1 lb. **Ground Turkey**
2 cans (10 3/4 oz. ea.) **Cream of Mushroom Soup**
1 cup grated **Longhorn Cheese**
1 cup grated **Monterey Jack Cheese**
1 medium **Anaheim Chile**, seeded and diced
2/3 cup **Milk**
1/2 cup **Vegetable Oil**

Sauté ground turkey in small amount of oil in a skillet until brown. Remove from heat and drain. In a saucepan, combine soup and 1/2 cup of longhorn and jack cheeses. Heat over medium heat until cheese is melted. Add milk and continue to stir while mixture simmers for 5 minutes. Stir in the green chiles and cover. Let simmer for an additional 10 minutes. Add turkey.

Meanwhile, soften tortillas by dipping each into hot vegetable oil for a few seconds per side. Drain on paper towels and stack.

Add just enough of the turkey mixture to cover the bottom of a shallow baking dish. Place a layer of corn tortillas on the top of the mixture. Add another layer of the turkey mixture and sprinkle with cheese. Repeat layering process until all ingredients are used. Top with cheese. Bake at 350 degrees for 25 to 30 minutes, until cheese bubbles. Serves 6.

Green River Baked Beans

1 can (15 oz.) **Pork and Beans**
1/2 cup **Barbecue Sauce**
2 tbsp. **Brown Sugar**
1/2 cup chopped **Onion**
1/2 cup grated **Cheddar Cheese**
6 **Bacon Strips**

Combine all ingredients, except for half of the cheese and half of the bacon strips, in a casserole dish. Place bacon strips across the top. Bake in 350 degree oven for 20 minutes or until the bacon is done. Garnish with remaining cheese and serve. Serves 4.

Double Sweet Potatoes

3 cups **Cooked Sweet Potatoes**, mashed
1/2 tsp. **Salt**
1/3 cup **Butter**
1 tsp. **Vanilla**
1/2 cup **Sugar**
2 **Eggs**, lightly beaten
1/2 cup **Sweet Milk**

Topping:

1 cup **Brown Sugar**
1 cup chopped **Nuts**
1/3 cup **Flour**

Mix sweet potatoes, salt, butter, vanilla, sugar, eggs, and milk together and place in a greased casserole dish. Mix topping ingredients together and sprinkle over potato mixture. Bake at 350 degrees for 35 minutes.

Serve warm, as a side dish or a dessert. Serves 4.

Piñon Nut Rice

1 cup chopped **Celery**
1 **Onion**, chopped
1 cup sliced fresh **Mushrooms**
2 tbsp. **Olive Oil**
3 cups **Brown Rice,** cooked
1 cup **Water**
2 tbsp. diced **Green Chiles**
1 cup chopped **Piñon Nuts**

Sauté celery, onion and mushrooms in oil. Add rice, water, green chiles and piñon nuts. Pour mixture into a greased baking dish and bake at 350 degrees for 30 minutes. Serve hot, garnished with sour cream. Serves 4.

Mini Frittatas

1 pkg. **Frozen Chopped Spinach**
1 cup chopped **Mushrooms**
2 tbsp. minced **Shallots**
2 tbsp. **Butter**
1 cup **Ricotta Cheese**
3/4 cup grated **Parmesan Cheese**
1 tsp. **Dried Oregano**
1 tsp. **Dried Basil**
1 tsp. **Salt**
1 tsp. **Pepper**
2 **Eggs**
4 slices **Prosciutto Ham**, cut to fit muffin cups
1 cup **Sour Cream**

First cook the frozen spinach according to the directions on the package and then drain. Sauté the mushrooms and shallots in butter until tender. In a medium bowl, mix the ricotta and Parmesan cheeses, herbs and salt and pepper. Stir in the eggs.

Butter 24 one-inch mini muffin cups. Lay sliced ham on the bottom of each cup. Spoon the cheese mixture into the cups. Bake at 375 degrees for 20 minutes or until the frittatas are golden on top. Let them cool for 10 minutes, then gently loosen them from the pan.

Serve warm with a dab of sour cream on top. Serves 4.

El Tovar Chili

This chili is a favorite treat of the patrons of the El Tovar Hotel,
especially on cold winter days!

1 1/2 lbs. **Filet Mignon**, diced
1 lb. **Pork Loin**, diced
1 **White Onion**, finely diced
1 **Jalapeño Pepper**, finely chopped
1 tbsp. finely chopped **Fresh Garlic**
3 cans (12 oz. ea.) **Beer**
3 tbsp. **Chili Powder**
1 tbsp. **Paprika**
1 tbsp. **Ground Cumin**
1 tbsp. **Tabasco**®
1/2 cup diced **Tomatoes**
1/2 cup **Tomato Sauce**
Salt and **Pepper** to taste

Sauté the first four ingredients for 5 minutes. Then add the rest of the ingredients. Simmer for 2 to 3 hours on low heat.

Put an individual portion of chili into an oven proof bowl and top with Monterey Jack cheese. Run under broiler for a few moments until cheese has melted and is slightly brown.

Serving suggestion: Accompany with blue corn chips and a slice of cornbread.

Crab Potato Bake

4 large **Baked Potatoes**
1 can (7 oz.) **Crabmeat**
1 cup grated **Cheddar Cheese**
2 tsp. minced **Onion**
1 tbsp. **Butter**
1/3 tsp. **Cayenne Pepper**
1 tsp. **Lemon Juice**
1/2 cup **Milk**
1 tsp. **Salt**
1 tsp. **Pepper**
1 tsp. **Paprika**

Split the baked potatoes lengthwise and scoop out the insides. Mix potatoes with remaining ingredients (except paprika) in a large bowl. Refill the potato shells with the new mixture. Add a dash of paprika to the top of each. Set oven at 350 degrees and bake for 20 minutes. Serve with sour cream and salsa. Serves 4.

Bacon & Bean Casserole

3 cups **Pinto Beans**, cooked
1 cup **Canned Tomatoes**
1/2 cup chopped **Green Bell Peppers**
1 tbsp. **Garlic Salt**
1 cup chopped **Onion**
1 tsp. **Salt**
1 tsp. **Chili Powder**
4 strips **Bacon**

Combine all ingredients, except the bacon strips. Place in a large greased baking dish. Arrange the bacon strips over the top. Bake in a 350 degree oven for one hour. Garnish with sour cream and tortilla chips. Serves 4.

Canyon Formation

According to scientists, the Grand Canyon is the result of erosion—the natural powers of wind, rain, ice and the mighty Colorado River. It is believed that the ancient Colorado River began carving the canyon about 10 million years ago.

The oldest rocks of the Grand Canyon, the Braham and Vishnu Schist, are found at the bottom of Granite Gorge. Pressures deep within the earth created these rocks over 2,000 million years ago during the Precambrian era. Because of the pressure, the Colorado Plateau began rising upward. This caused the existing rivers that were once slow and gentle to become faster and more abrasive.

In addition to the harsh river, the elements of nature have been hard at work, too. The powerful qualities of heat, cold, rain and snow, coupled with the various types of rock formation, have combined to carve the canyon we witness today as this process continues.

For those who hike along the canyon walls, it is truly a walk back into time.

Breads

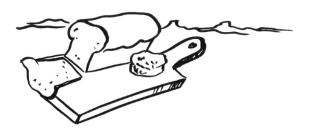

Anasazi Pumpkin Muffins

3 cups **Flour**
2 cups **Sugar**
1 tsp. **Baking Soda**
1 tsp. **Salt**
3 tsp. **Cinnamon**
2 cups **Pumpkin**
1 1/4 cups **Oil**
4 **Eggs**
1 cup **Pecans**

Sift together the flour, sugar, baking soda, salt and cinnamon. Mix the pumpkin, oil and eggs in a large bowl and add the sifted ingredients. Add the pecans and pour batter into muffin tins. Bake in a preheated oven at 350 degrees for 20 to 25 minutes. Makes 24 muffins.

Pineapple-Bran Muffins

2 cups **Boiling Water**
1 cup **Butter**
4 cups **Bran Cereal**
3 cups **Sugar**
4 **Eggs**
1 qt. **Buttermilk**
5 cups **Flour**
5 tsp. **Baking Soda**
1 tsp. **Salt**
1 cup **Pineapple Chunks**

Pour boiling water over butter and stir until butter is melted. Add bran cereal, sugar, eggs, and buttermilk and mix together. Add the flour, baking soda and salt. Mix throughly and then add the pineapple. Place batter in refrigerator overnight. Pour into muffin tins and bake in a 400 degree oven for 20 minutes. Makes 24 muffins.

Green Chile Bread

Serve this bread for breakfast, lunch or dinner!
It tastes great warm with butter or salsa!

1 cup **Cornmeal**
3/4 cup **Milk**
1/3 cup **Oil**
2 **Eggs**
1 can (13 oz.) **Creamed Corn**
1/4 cup grated **Cheddar Cheese**
1 can (4 oz.) **Green Chiles**
2 tsp. **Baking Soda**
1/2 tsp. **Salt**

Mix cornmeal, milk, oil and eggs together until smooth. Next add the corn, cheese, chiles, baking soda and salt. Bake in a 13 × 9 greased casserole dish at 325 degrees for 30 minutes.

Cowboy Cornbread

This is a large loaf of bread and can be "hot" due to the jalapeños,
serve with a warning... "Hot bread"!

3 boxes (14 oz. ea.) **CornBread Mix**
2 1/2 cups **Milk**
3 **Eggs**
1/2 cup **Oil**
2 cups grated **Cheddar Cheese**
1 can (13 oz) **Creamed Corn**
1 can (4 oz.) diced **Jalapeños**

Mix all ingredients in a large bowl until smooth. Pour into a greased and floured 13 × 9 × 2 loaf pan. Bake at 325 degrees for one hour.

Grand Canyon Coffeecake

3 cups **Flour**, sifted
3 tsp. **Baking Powder**
1 tsp. **Salt**
1/4 tsp. **Nutmeg**
1 tsp. **Cinnamon**
1 cup **Sugar**
1/4 cup **Butter**
2 **Eggs**
1 cup **Milk**
1/4 cup chopped **Piñon Nuts**
1/2 cup **Heavy Cream**, whipped

Sift dry ingredients together. Blend in butter and add unbeaten eggs and milk and stir until smooth. Add piñon nuts and stir. Pour mixture into well-greased round cake pan and cover with the following topping.

Topping:

1/4 cup **Butter**
1 cup **Brown Sugar**
3 tbsp. **Flour**
1 tsp. **Cinnamon**
1/8 tsp. **Salt**
1/2 cup chopped **Piñon Nuts**

Cream together the butter, brown sugar and flour. Add cinnamon and salt and stir. Spread mixture over top of coffeecake. Sprinkle with nuts. Bake at 375 degrees for 25 minutes. When the cake has cooled, split into layers and spread the whipped cream between the layers. Place layers back together, cut into individual portions and serve.

Apple Biscuits

2 cups **Flour**, sifted
1 tsp. **Salt**
4 tsp. **Baking Powder**
4 tbsp. **Shortening**
3/4 cup **Milk**
3 **Cooking Apples**
Sugar
Cinnamon
1/4 cup **Butter**

In a large bowl, mix flour, salt, baking powder, shortening and milk until smooth. Peel and core apples and cut into quarters. Fill greased muffin pans half full with dough. Press an apple quarter into the center of each muffin cup. Sprinkle with sugar and cinnamon. Put a small amount of butter on top. Bake in a 350 degree oven for 10 minutes, or until apples start to liquefy. Serve with apple juice and honey. Makes 12 biscuits.

Cheese Biscuits

2 cups **Flour**
2 tsp. **Baking Powder**
1/2 tsp. **Salt**
1/2 cup grated **Cheddar Cheese**
2 tbsp. **Shortening**
1 cup **Milk**

In a large bowl, sift flour, baking powder and salt together. Add cheese and blend in shortening. Add milk gradually. Drop from tablespoon onto baking sheet. Bake in hot oven (400 degrees) for 5 minutes, then reduce heat to 300 degrees and continue baking for 10 minutes. Makes 8 biscuits.

Canyon Wildlife

The Grand Canyon area teems with wildlife and you will see your share of it as you hike a trail or drive along the rim roads. Early mornings or late afternoons are the best times to view animals.

Do not feed the wildlife, no matter how tame they may appear. Animals expecting handouts can become very aggressive and have been known to bite visitors. Please resist the temptation to feed them.

The curious and clever Abert squirrel resides at the South Rim of the canyon. The black-bellied Kaibab squirrel, is found only on the North Rim. You may be fortunate enough to spot a beautiful mule deer, so named for its long ears. Or hear the song of the silver-gray coyote as he moves about searching for food over this vast terrain.

There are seven types of hawks and eagles soaring through the skies. The red-tailed hawk is often visible as it glides gently upon the air currents. Or, you may see the glorious golden eagle with its wing span of up to six feet. This powerful bird carries rodents and even baby bighorn sheep in its talons to take back to its young ones in their nest.

Keep a watchful eye out for the ringtail cat, a night mammal who resembles a raccoon and is found near the Colorado River. Bighorn sheep can be seen too, along the craggy edges of the canyon walls.

Many reptiles live at the canyon, including the Grand Canyon rattlesnake, chuckwalla and collared lizard.

Desserts

Piñon Nut Apple Crisp

6 large **Red Delicious Apples**, peeled and sliced
1/4 cup diced **Piñon Nuts**
20 **Dates**, softened, diced
1 cup **Apple Juice**
1/2 cup **Oil**
1/4 cup **Water**
2 cups **Quick-Cooking Rolled Oats**
1 cup **Whole Wheat Pastry Flour**
1/2 tsp. **Salt**

Place the apples, nuts and dates in a large baking dish. Thoroughly mix the balance of the ingredients together in a large bowl. Place this mixture over the apples and dates. Bake in a 350 degree oven for 45 minutes or until top becomes golden brown.

Serve while still warm with ice cream and enjoy!

Apple Juice Pie

6 cups **Apples**, peeled and sliced
1 can (12 oz.) **Frozen Apple Juice**, thawed
2 tbsp. **Cornstarch**
1 tsp. **Fennel Seed**
1/8 tsp. **Salt**
1 tsp. **Vanilla**
1 tsp. **Cinnamon**
2 prepared 9-inch **Pie Crusts**

Place all ingredients in a saucepan, stir and simmer until thickened. Pour mixture into a 9-inch unbaked pie shell and cover with a top crust. Bake at 375 degrees for 30 minutes.

Grandma's Cookies

Send a dozen of these cookies to someone you love.

1/2 cup **Oil**
1 1/2 cups **Dates**, pitted
1 tsp. **Vanilla**
1 tsp. **Salt**
1 cup **Wheat Germ**
1 cup **Whole Wheat Pastry Flour**
1 cup **Quick-Cooking Rolled Oats**
1/2 cup **Water**

In a large bowl, combine oil and dates and mix to a consistency of smooth butter. Add the balance of the ingredients except water and mix thoroughly. Add water sparingly until mixture can be formed into a ball. Roll out and cut into cookie shapes. Bake on a lightly oiled cookie sheet at 350 degrees for 15 minutes or until cookies are browned. Cool on a wire rack.

Canyon Date Cookies

1 cup **Dates**, pitted
1/2 cup **Water**
1 cup **Apples**, peeled, shredded
3/4 cup **Oil**
1/2 tsp. **Salt**
1/2 cup chopped **Piñon Nuts**
1 tsp. **Vanilla**
3 cups **Quick-Cooking Rolled Oats**

Combine dates and water in saucepan. On medium heat, mix and mash the dates until they are smooth. Add the apple and oil and beat together. Add the balance of ingredients and mix well. Let mixture stand for 15 minutes at room temperature. Use a teaspoon to drop cookie dough onto ungreased cookie sheet. Bake in oven at 375 for 20 minutes or until cookies are brown. Makes approximately 3 dozen cookies.

Carrot Brownies

1/2 cup **Butter**
1 1/2 cups **Light Brown Sugar**
2 **Eggs**
2 cups **All-Purpose Flour**, sifted
2 tsp. **Baking Powder**
1/2 tsp. **Salt**
2 cups grated **Carrots**
1/2 cup chopped **Walnuts**

In a large saucepan melt the butter. Add the brown sugar and stir until sugar is melted. Remove from heat and beat in the eggs. Add the flour, baking powder, salt and carrots. Mix thoroughly and then pour into two 8 × 8 × 2 greased pans. Sprinkle the chopped walnuts over the tops of each pan. Bake in a pre-heated oven at 350 degrees for 30 minutes. When cooled, cut into squares and serve.

Strawberry Pie

2 **Egg Whites**
1 tbsp. **Lemon Juice**
1/2 cup **Sugar**
1 pkg. (10 oz.) frozen **Strawberries**, thawed
1 ctn. (8 oz.) **Whipped Non-Dairy Topping**
1 **Graham Cracker Crust**

In a large bowl mix egg whites, lemon juice, sugar and strawberries. Beat with mixer for 2 minutes at high speed. Add the whipped topping and combine. Pour mixture into the graham cracker crust and freeze for 2 hours or more.

Cactus Fruit Sauce

1/4 cup **Honey**
1/2 tsp. **Salt**
1 **Lime**, juiced
1 1/2 tbsp. **Cornstarch**
1 cup **Prickly Pear Fruit**, puréed
1 tbsp. **Butter**

Blend the honey, salt, lime juice, cornstarch and prickly pear fruit in a saucepan. Place over medium heat and cook and stir mixture until it begins to thicken. Add the butter and heat for 5 minutes on low heat. Serve this sauce warm over ice cream for a cactus treat!

Sweet Potato Cake

2 1/2 cups **Self-Rising Flour**, sifted
1 tsp. **Cinnamon**
1 tsp. **Nutmeg**
1 1/2 cups **Cooking Oil**
2 cups **Sugar**
4 **Eggs**
1/4 cup **Hot Water**
1 1/2 cups grated raw **Sweet Potatoes**
1 cup chopped **Piñon Nuts**
1 tsp. **Vanilla**
1/2 cup **Raisins**

First sift flour, cinnamon and nutmeg in a mixing bowl. In a separate large bowl, combine cooking oil and sugar. Beat in eggs one at a time. Add the hot water. Fold in flour mixture. Stir in the sweet potatoes, nuts, vanilla and raisins. Mix thoroughly.

Pre-heat oven to 350 degrees. Grease and lightly flour three 8-inch round layer cake pans. Pour batter into pans and bake at 350 degrees for 30 minutes. Cool to room temperature and frost with Coconut Frosting.

Coconut Frosting

1 can (14 oz.) **Evaporated Milk**
1 cup **Sugar**
1 stick **Butter**
3 **Egg Yolks**
1 tsp. **Vanilla**
1 1/2 cups **Coconut Flakes**

Combine the evaporated milk, sugar, butter and egg yolks in a saucepan. Cook on medium heat, stirring constantly, until mixture thickens (about 25 minutes). Remove from heat, add vanilla and coconut flakes and stir. Spread frosting on one layer, top with second layer and frost. Add top layer and frost again. Serve with your favorite cup of coffee and enjoy!

Rhubarb Pie

Rhubarb can be slightly bitter, but the sugar smooths out the taste and makes this a delicious dessert!

1 single shell **Pie Crust**
4 cups **Rhubarb**, chunks
1 1/2 cups **Sugar**
3 tbsp. **Flour**
1 **Egg**, beaten
1 cup **Sweet Cream**

Place crust in a pie pan. Blend rhubarb on low in a food processor until semi-smooth. Pour rhubarb into pie crust. Mix sugar, flour, egg and sweet cream. Pour mixture over rhubarb. Bake in a pre-heated oven at 350 degrees for 30 minutes or until pie is thick and the crust is browned. Let cool and serve with ice cream.

Banana Date Cake

1 3/4 cups **Flour**, sifted
1 tsp. **Baking Soda**
1/2 tsp. **Salt**
1/2 cup **Butter**
1 cup **Brown Sugar**
1/2 cup **Sugar**
2 **Eggs**, separated
1 tsp. **Vanilla**
1/2 cup **Buttermilk**
1 cup **Bananas**, mashed
1/2 cup pitted and chopped **Dates**
1/2 cup chopped **Walnuts**

Grease and flour a 9-inch square cake pan. Sift the flour with the baking soda and salt. Set aside. Cream the butter until it's very light and then add brown and white sugars, beating until the mixture is light and fluffy. Beat in the egg yolks and vanilla. Combine buttermilk with mashed bananas. Add sifted dry ingredients to the butter mixture alternately with the banana mixture. Blend in dates and nuts. Beat egg whites until stiff and fold them in last. Turn batter into the prepared pan and bake in a 350 degree oven for 45 minutes. Cool and frost with Butter Frosting.

Butter Frosting

2 tbsp. **Butter**
1 cup **Confectioners' Sugar**
2 tbsp. **Orange Juice**

Soften butter and mix gradually with sugar and orange juice. Beat until mixture is soft and creamy. Spread over top of cake and serve.

Chocolate Canyon Bread Pudding

The chocolate chips melt and ooze into every crack and crevice, guaranteeing chocolate in every bite!

2 1/2 cups **Bread Cubes**
2 1/2 cups **Milk**
4 tbsp. **Butter**
1/2 cup **Honey**
1/4 tsp. **Salt**
2 **Eggs,** beaten
1 tsp. **Vanilla**
1/2 cup **Raisins**
1/2 cup **Chocolate Chips**

Place bread cubes in a large bowl. Heat milk to a boil and then pour over bread. Let set for five minutes. Add butter, honey and salt and mix well. Let cool for several minutes. Mix in eggs, vanilla, raisins and chocolate chips. Pour mixture into greased baking dish. Place dish in a pan of hot water and bake in oven at 350 degrees for one hour, or until pudding is firm.

Let cool for 10 minutes before serving.

Date Pudding

1/2 cup **Sugar**
1 **Egg**, beaten
1 cup pitted and chopped **Dates**
1/4 cup **Flour**
1/2 tsp. **Salt**
1/2 tsp. **Baking Powder**
1/2 cup chopped **Walnuts**

Mix sugar and egg thoroughly. Add dates, flour, salt, baking powder and walnuts. Put into a greased, shallow baking dish. Bake at 350 degrees for 30 minutes. Serve warm with a dollop of whipped cream on top.

Indian Corn Pudding

4 cups **Milk**
1/2 cup **Cornmeal**
1 tsp. **Salt**
1/4 cup **Corn Syrup**
1/2 cup **Sugar**
1/2 tsp. **Cinnamon**
2 tbsp. **Butter**

In a saucepan, combine milk, cornmeal and salt. Cook at medium heat for about 15 minutes and then remove from heat. Add syrup and sugar. Stir in cinnamon and butter. Put into a greased baking dish and bake in a 350 degree oven for 1 1/2 to 2 hours. Serve warm.

Piñon Nut Squares

3/4 cup **Flour**
1/2 tsp. **Salt**
1/2 tsp. **Cinnamon**
1/4 tsp. **Baking Soda**
1 cup **Quick-Cooking Rolled Oats**
1 **Egg**
1/3 cup **White Sugar**
1/3 cup **Brown Sugar**, firmly packed
1/2 cup softened **Butter**
1 tsp. **Vanilla**
1 cup chopped **Piñon Nuts**

1/2 cup **Raisins**

Sift flour, salt, cinnamon and baking soda together. Mix oats into dry ingredients. In a large bowl, beat egg, both sugars, butter, and vanilla until fluffy. Mix in dry ingredients. Stir in piñon nuts and raisins. Drop by tablespoonfuls onto greased cookie sheet. Bake in center of 375 degree oven for 10 to 12 minutes. Makes 3 dozen cookies.

Flan

1 3/4 cups **Sugar**
3 **Egg Whites**
8 **Egg Yolks**
2 cans **Evaporated Milk**
2 tsp. **Vanilla**

Melt one cup of the sugar over very low heat. Pour into a 2-quart casserole dish, tilting to make sure that melted sugar covers bottom and sides of the pan completely. Allow to cool. Beat the egg whites and yolks together. Add milk, the remaining sugar and vanilla. Pour into the sugar-lined mold.

Place mold in a pan of water in the oven at 350 degrees for about one hour, or until a knife inserted into the center comes out clean. Cool for a few minutes, then turn upside down and turn out onto a plate. Serve warm or refrigerate.

Chile Pepper Jelly

1 cup **Green Bell Pepper,** chopped
1/2 cup **Fresh Green Chiles,** chopped
6 1/2 cups **Sugar**
1 1/2 cups **Apple Cider Vinegar**
6 oz. **Pectin**
6 drops **Green Food Coloring**

Place chopped peppers in a blender. Blend on medium speed for 1 minute. Combine the sugar and cider vinegar with the blended peppers in a large saucepan. Bring this mixture to a boil. Remove from heat and let stand for about 5 minutes. Add the pectin and food coloring and stir together. Store in refrigerator. Yields 2 to 3 pints of jelly.

Serve over cream cheese with crackers on the side for a tingling treat.

The El Tovar Hotel

The hotels and lodges of the Grand Canyon are steeped in history and rich in tradition. The El Tovar Hotel was built in 1902, designed by a Chicago architect. Styled similar to a Swiss chalet and a Norway villa, it is built on concrete and rubble masonry with a wood frame structure.

The interior is supported by a peeled log framework topped with decorative corbels throughout the mezzanine. By the time it was completed in January, 1905, the name had changed from "Bright Angel Tavern" to "El Tovar" in honor of Pedro de Tovar of the Coronado Expedition.

At a cost of $250,000, the El Tovar was a very elegant and modern hotel for the times. The hotel had electric lights powered by its own coal-fired generator and its own greenhouse for fresh fruits and vegetables. A chicken house supplied fresh eggs and fresh milk came from the hotel's own dairy herd.

Inside the El Tovar were a barbershop, solarium, amusement room, club room, and art and music rooms. These rooms are no longer a part of the hotel, but the dining room with its large picture windows overlooking the canyon still remains. A cocktail lounge and a large porch on the north side were added in the 1950s, and more recently, a gift shop and a lounge complete with fireplace.

Today the El Tovar Hotel continues to attract visitors from around the world.

Index

If you love cookbooks, then you'll love these too

Salsa Lovers Cookbook
More than 180 recipes for salsa, dips, salads, appetizers and more!
$9.95

Quick-n-Easy Mexican Recipes
Make your favorite Mexican dishes in record time! Excellent tacos, tostadas, enchiladas and more!
$9.95

Chip and Dip Lovers Cookbook
Easy and colorful recipes from Southwestern salsas to quick appetizer dips!
$9.95

Tortilla Lovers' Cookbook
Celebrate the tortilla w more than 100 easy recipes for break lunch, dinner, appetizer desserts, too!
$9.95

Chili Lovers Cookbook
Prize-winning recipes for chili, with or without beans. Plus a variety of taste-tempting foods made with flavorful chile peppers.
$9.95

Arizona Cookbook
A collection of more than 350 authentic Arizona recipes. Including Indian, Mexican. and Western foods.
$9.95

New Mexico Cookbook
This unique book explores the age-old recipes that are rich with the heritage of New Mexico.
$9.95

Easy RV Recipe
Easy recipes for th traveling cook. Ov 200 recipes to mak in your RV, camper houseboat.
$9.95

Easy Recipes for Wild Game
More than 200 "wild" recipes for large and small game, wild fowl and fish.
$9.95

Apple Lovers Cookbook
What's more American than eating apple pie? Try these 150 favorite recipes for appetizers, main and side dishes, muffins, pies, salads, beverages and preserves.
$9.95

Pumpkin Lovers Cookbook
More than 175 recipes for soups, breads, muffins, pies, cakes, cheesecakes, cookies and even ice cream! Carving tips, trivia and more.
$9.95

Mexican Family Favorites Recip
250 authentic, homes recipes for tacos, tam. menudo, enchiladas, ros, salsas, carne seca, rellenos, and guacam
$9.95

www.GoldenWestPublishers.com